A STUDENT'S DICTIONARY OF PSYCHOLOGY

David A. Statt

Psychology Press
Taylor & Francis Group

HOVE AND NEW YORK

First published 2003
by Psychology Press
27 Church Road, Hove, East Sussex, BN3 2FA

Simultaneously published in the USA and Canada
by Psychology Press
29 West 35th Street, New York, NY 10001

Psychology Press is a part of the Taylor & Francis Group

© 2003 David A. Statt

Typeset in Times by RefineCatch Limited, Bungay, Suffolk
Printed and bound in Great Britain by
TJ International, Padstow, Cornwall
Cover design by Leigh Hurlock

British Library Cataloguing in Publication Data
A catalogue record for this book is available from the British Library

Library of Congress Cataloging in Publication Data
Statt, David A., 1942–
A students dictionary of psychology/David A. Statt.—1st ed.
    p.   cm.
ISBN 1-84169-341-3 — ISBN 1-84169-342-1 (pbk.)
1. Psychology—Dictionaries.   I. Title.
BF31.S64 2003
150'.3—dc21   2003012043

ISBN 1–84169–342–1 (pbk)
ISBN 1–84169–341–3 (hbk)

To Mike Forster,
for auld lang syne

ACKNOWLEDGEMENT

The author and publisher are very grateful to Palgrave Macmillan for their kind permission to reproduce Figure 2, Attitude, from *Understanding the Consumer: A Psychological Interpretation* by David A. Statt.

A

ablation   A surgical procedure in which BRAIN tissue is systematically destroyed and often removed.

abnormal or **atypical psychology**   The study of individuals
who differ from the NORM, such as those with mental disorders. The
term "abnormal" is often used as a way of labelling people whose
behaviour is unusual. See LABELLING THEORY.

abnormality   Behaviour that is considered to deviate from the
NORM (statistical or social), or ideal mental health. It is dysfunctional
because it is harmful or causes distress to the individual or others
and so is considered to be a failure to function adequately.
Abnormality is characterised by the fact that it is an undesirable
state that causes severe impairment in the personal and social functioning of the individual, and often causes the person great anguish
depending on how much insight they have into their illness.

abreaction   The relief of tension that patients experience in
PSYCHOANALYSIS when they relive a conflict or trauma that they
had repressed. See also CATHARSIS.

absolute morality   This is based on the notion that the ends cannot justify the means; some acts are basically immoral regardless of
the consequences they produce.

absolute threshold   The point at which a stimulus can just be
picked up by the sense organs.

absolutism (in moral development)   According to PIAGET, a
concern with rules about the world, as reflected in a child's play,
begins around the age of 5. At this stage, children have a blind faith
in the rules and the ideas of right and wrong given them by their

1

parents. Each child regards his or her parents as the ultimate arbiters of these rules which they perceive as being quite absolute, subject to no arguments, compromises, or changes of any kind.

accommodation (1) In PIAGET's theory, the process of changing existing schemas or creating new schemas because new information cannot be ASSIMILATED. (2) The process of adjusting the shape of the lens of the eye to ensure that images are focused on the retina.

acculturation The process by which people learn the assumptions, beliefs, and behaviour patterns of a CULTURE, either as children growing up in a certain time and place or as adults moving from one culture to another.

acculturation strategy The approach adopted by members of ethnic groups, involving decisions about preserving their own cultural identity and about contact with other cultural groups.

achieved status A term for describing a position that someone has achieved in society by his or her own efforts. Contrasted with ASCRIBED STATUS.

achievement, need for See NEED FOR ACHIEVEMENT.

acoustic coding Encoding words in terms of their sound using information stored in LONG-TERM MEMORY.

acquired characteristic Originally used in GENETICS to describe a change that occurs in the physical structure of an organism as a result of its own activities or its interaction with the environment, i.e., a characteristic (like a bodybuilder's biceps) that is not INNATE. There has long been an argument as to whether acquired characteristics can be genetically transferred to offspring (see LAMARCKIAN-ISM). Nowadays this argument is generally considered a loser, although interest in it may still revive. In PSYCHOLOGY, skills acquired by learning (like reading and writing) are sometimes referred to as acquired characteristics.

acquired drive Sometimes used of MOTIVATION, the arousal or satisfaction of which has been learned.

acquired status See ACHIEVED STATUS.

acting out In PSYCHOANALYSIS, a term for the behaviour of a patient who has to act on a powerful and deep-rooted impulse, and is unable to reflect on it and talk about it instead.

action slips Actions that occur, but were not intended. Often described as absent-minded behaviour, such as putting teabags into the kettle instead of the teapot.

active sleep   A term used to refer to REM SLEEP.

actor–observer effect   The tendency for actors to attribute their actions to situational factors, whereas observers attribute them to internal/external dispositional factors. See FUNDAMENTAL ATTRIBUTION ERROR.

actualising tendency   Sometimes employed by humanistic psychologists in referring to the basic MOTIVATION of people to support and develop the self. See SELF-ACTUALISATION.

acuity   Literally, sharpness. Used in relation to the senses, e.g., visual acuity.

adaptation   Originally a biological term used to describe physical or behavioural changes that increased an organism's chances of survival. Used in PSYCHOLOGY to describe responses to changes in the environment, e.g., DARK–LIGHT ADAPTATION, or where the changed expectations of their society demand some kind of social adaptation in people's behaviour. See also ADJUSTMENT.

adaptation level   The concept that an organism will perceive and interpret a particular stimulus within the context or frame of reference in which it was previously learned.

adaptation time   The time taken for a sense organ to adapt to a stimulus, as measured by the time elapsed between the start of a steady stimulus and the cessation of any further response to it.

adaptive   The extent to which a behaviour increases the reproductive potential of an individual and survival of its GENES.

addiction   Physiological and psychological dependence on a drug in order to function. It implies both a physiological and psychological adaptation to an altered normality.

adjustment   Similar to ADAPTATION, especially in a social context, but usually implies a greater purposiveness and awareness on the part of the individual faced with environmental demands.

Adler, Alfred (1870–1937)   An early disciple of FREUD who founded his own movement in 1911, the first of Freud's major followers to break away. Adler disagreed with Freud's emphasis on the importance of sexuality to the human condition, preferring to stress the drive for power and the need to compensate for deficiencies experienced by people in certain areas of their personality—the source of the famous INFERIORITY COMPLEX.

adolescence   Usually defined as the period of human development between the onset of puberty at around 12 years and the attainment of physical adult maturity at around 21 years; i.e., a biological definition. Emotional, moral and intellectual development may not occur on the same time schedule. The interrelation of these different types of development gives this period its psychological importance. Adolescence is unique to our kind of society. Anthropologists and historians have found societies in which the onset of puberty is taken to mark the full transition from childhood to adulthood, with no other period of preparation being thought necessary.

adrenal glands   The endocrine glands that are located adjacent to, and covering, the upper part of the kidneys.

adrenaline   One of the HORMONES (along with NORADRENALINE) produced by the ADRENAL GLANDS, which increases arousal by activating the sympathetic nervous system and reducing activity in the parasympathetic system.

aesthesiometer   An instrument for quantifying skin sensitivity to touch by measuring the smallest distance between two points of contact on the skin where the person can perceive each of them separately rather than as a single stimulus.

aetiology   The study of the causes of a disease or disorder.

affect   Widely used in psychology for feeling and emotion.

affectionless psychopathy   A condition where individuals appear to experience little guilt or emotion, lack normal affection, and are unable to form long-term relationships.

afferent   The process of carrying information from the sense organs through the nerves *to* the brain. Contrasted with EFFERENT.

affiliation, need for   See NEED FOR AFFILIATION.

affordances   In Gibson's theory, the possible uses of objects, which are claimed to be given directly in the sensory information provided by the stimulus.

after-image   A visual impression that persists after the stimulus has been removed, e.g., when the eyes are closed after looking at a bright light.

age-grading   The process of dividing the members of a society into groups according to their ages, applying labels to these groups (infants, teenagers, senior citizens, etc.) and expecting the members of each group to behave in certain characteristic (or "normal") ways. This process is perhaps most clearly seen when people do not behave in the manner expected of them. For example, a child in solemn mood may be described as a "little old man", or a middle-aged person whooping it up may be having a "second childhood".

4

Age-grading is found in all societies, although the gradations and the expectations of behaviour that accompany it vary enormously.

ageing Usually defined as the process of growing old and the study of old age (see GERONTOLOGY). However, ageing is a lifelong business. It is generally accepted that heredity plays an important part in determining length of life and perhaps also the quality of health in old age. Other important factors may be the SELF-IMAGE formed in early life which helps shape one's behaviour and attitudes at different ages, and early conceptions of what being old is, or should be, like.

ageism Like racism and sexism, ageism is discrimination against people because of an attribute arbitrarily determined—in this case by birth-age.

agentic state A state of feeling controlled by an authority figure, and therefore lacking a sense of personal responsibility.

agnosia A failure of PERCEPTION caused by BRAIN DAMAGE. The sufferer is unable to recognise familiar objects or make sense out of sensory information.

agoraphobia PHOBIA about open spaces.

aha reaction A sudden insight, the kind that often accompanies the exclamation "aha!". It is used to describe the moment when the solution to a problem appears or the disparate elements of a situation suddenly add up to a meaningful pattern. See GESTALT and GESTALT PSYCHOLOGY.

AI See ARTIFICIAL INTELLIGENCE.

alexia Word blindness. The loss, through BRAIN DAMAGE, of the ability to read.

algorithms Step-by-step procedures that will definitely solve a problem (e.g., a knitting pattern). Compare with HEURISTICS.

alienation A term with various shades of psychological and sociological meaning all of which refer in common to feelings of being estranged, separated, and powerless, whether in relation to oneself, to nature, to other people, to wealth and the means of production in a society, or else to society as a whole. Compare with EFFICACY.

allele One of the two (or more) forms of a GENE. CHROMOSOMES are paired, and at the same position on each chromosome is a gene for a particular characteristic such as eye colour. These two genes are called alleles.

all-or-none principle Used in physiological psychology to describe the way a nerve responds to stimulation. Either the stimulus is inadequate and the nerve does not respond at all or it responds to its maximum capacity.

alpha bias   The tendency to exaggerate differences between the sexes.

alpha rhythm   The type of BRAIN WAVES found in adults when they are resting. They have an average frequency of ten per second.

alter ego   A literary term, meaning "the other I", for a person who seems to exemplify another version of oneself.

altercasting   Term used by some social psychologists to describe the process of trying to get someone to play the role you want them to.

altered states of consciousness   Situations in which one's subjective experience is different from normal waking consciousness. These alterations can be caused by drugs or stimulants or emotional upheaval or a combination of these. Religious ecstasy is a common type of altered state and is often accompanied by visions and other mystical experiences.

alternative hypothesis   The alternative to the NULL HYPOTHESIS. That is, the findings in a study are not due to chance and do reflect a true difference, effect or relationship. In an EXPERIMENT this would be known as the EXPERIMENTAL HYPOTHESIS.

altruism   A form of PRO-SOCIAL BEHAVIOUR that is costly to the altruist, and which is motivated by the wish to help another individual.

Alzheimer's disease   A degenerative form of DEMENTIA whose symptoms are similar to senile dementia but which can occur in middle age.

ambiguity, tolerance for   See TOLERANCE FOR AMBIGUITY.

ambiguous figures   A drawing that appears to change as you look at it and become something else. The two figures alternate automatically as the perceptual system recognises first one then the other. It is not possible to perceive both at the same time (Figure 1).

ambivalence   Tendency to oscillate between opposing types of behaviour, opinions, and, especially, feelings about someone.

amnesia   Partial loss of LONG-TERM MEMORY, usually caused by BRAIN DAMAGE. See also DISSOCIATIVE DISORDERS and REPRESSION.

amnesia, infantile   See INFANTILE AMNESIA.

amygdalotomy   A form of PSYCHOSURGERY where the amygdala, which is the part of the BRAIN involved in anger, is destroyed using strong electrical currents.

anaclitic depression   A severe form of DEPRESSION in infants who experience prolonged separations from their mothers. The term

Figure 1 Ambiguous figures

"anaclitic" means "arising from emotional dependency on another".

anaesthesia Loss of sensitivity to stimulation which may be total (as when a general anaesthetic is given before surgery) or local. A local anaesthetic may also be given for minor surgery. Local anaesthesia that is not artificially induced in this way is psychological in origin. It may be known as glove or shoe or stocking anaesthesia to indicate the part of the body affected. This kind of anaesthesia is a symptom of HYSTERIA.

anal stage According to FREUD this is the second stage in an infant's life, when he or she is mainly concerned with the pleasure received from the anus and its function. Anxiety caused by toilet training may overlay the infant's pleasure. As with all of Freud's stages, excessive frustration or satisfaction at the anal stage may leave a person fixated on it, with the eventual result that, as an adult, he or she may exhibit an "anal" character typified by obstinacy, tidiness, and miserliness.

analogies test A widely used type of mental test which asks the subject to complete the fourth term, e.g., "champagne is to France as caviar is to . . ."

analysand Someone undergoing PSYCHOANALYSIS.

analysis See PSYCHOANALYSIS.

7

analysis of variance Statistical technique for determining whether the differences found in a DEPENDENT VARIABLE in an experiment are greater than can be expected by chance. It is used for making simultaneous comparisons between two or more group MEANS.

analyst See PSYCHOANALYST.

anchoring Forming social representations by relating new ideas closely to existing knowledge.

androcentric bias A bias in favour of males. An androcentric theory is based on research data on males and then applied to all human behaviour.

androgynous Tendency of a male body to show female physical characteristics. Sometimes used the other way around.

animism The belief that inanimate natural objects (like rocks or rivers) are animate living things, or contain souls or spiritual forces.

anisogamy Sexual reproduction in which the gametes of the two sexes are dissimilar, for example the human ovum (egg cell) and sperm.

anomie Term introduced by the French 19th-century sociologist Emile Durkheim to describe a condition of society where SOCIAL NORMS are breaking down and people may become confused both about their place in that society and about their sense of identity in general.

anorexia nervosa An eating disorder characterised by the individual being severely underweight; 85% or less than expected for size and height. There is also ANXIETY, as the anorexic has an intense fear of becoming fat and a distorted BODY IMAGE. The individual does not have an accurate perception of their body size, seeing themself as "normal" when they are in fact significantly underweight, and they may minimise the dangers of being severely underweight.

ANS See AUTONOMIC NERVOUS SYSTEM.

anthropocentric Acting on the unquestioned assumption that mankind is the centre of the universe.

anthropology The study of the different physical and cultural conditions of mankind.

anthropomorphism The tendency to see human qualities in non-humans, like gods or animals.

anticipatory socialisation An aspect of SOCIALISATION where an individual prepares for a future role by taking on values and attitudes associated with the role before actually occupying it. Used in work and consumer psychology.

anti-social behaviour   Behaviour that harms or injures another person.

anti-social personality   Characterised by lack of conscience. Such a person has not internalised the values of his society and seems to feel no GUILT or ANXIETY in behaving criminally, and even committing murder. Often accompanied by a tendency to gratify needs impulsively that results in chronic conflict with society. Also referred to as a "PSYCHOPATH" or "psychopathic personality".

anxiety   A term used with many shades of meaning and in many different areas of psychology. It is generally held to be an unpleasant emotional state resulting from STRESS or conflict and characterised by fear and apprehension. If the fear and apprehension are vague and diffuse and not attached to a specific object, or if they seem excessive, the anxiety is considered NEUROTIC.

aphasia   Loss of ability to use language (especially the ability to speak) because of BRAIN DAMAGE.

apparent motion   The illusion of movement created when similar stationary stimuli are presented in rapid succession. See PHI PHENOMENON.

apperception   The final stage in the process of PERCEPTION where something is in the forefront of one's attention and is clearly recognised or understood.

applied psychology   The term normally used for those areas of psychology that attempt to apply psychological theories and findings to particular issues of everyday life, such as counselling, education, industrial relations, etc. Can also be used to describe the contributions of psychologists in a wide variety of more unusual areas, such as designing instrument panels for spaceships and assisting police in dealing with hostage takers.

appraisal   (1) An evaluation of how someone has performed in a job. (2) Where an individual evaluates a situation for possible STRESS.

approach–approach conflict   Caused by having to choose between two desirable objects or goals.

approach–avoidance conflict   Caused by being confronted with an object or goal that is at the same time both attractive and unattractive (like delicious Chinese food that gives you heartburn).

9

aptitude   The potential for acquiring a skill or ability after some training.

aptitude test   A test that tries to predict a person's capacity for acquiring a certain skill or ability.

arachnophobia   PHOBIA of spiders.

archetype   JUNG's term for the contents of what he called the collective unconscious, a set of behaviour patterns that were supposedly passed on from generation to generation as the common heritage of mankind. Evidence for this archetype, according to Jung, lay in the similarity of symbols in different cultures across time and place for fertility, birth, death, and so on.

arcuate fasciculus   A bundle of axons connecting BROCA'S AREA with WERNICKE'S AREA in the BRAIN; damage to this bundle of axons can cause CONDUCTION APHASIA.

Army Alpha Tests   The first INTELLIGENCE TEST to be used en masse—by the United States army during World War I. It was designed for literate English speakers.

arousal/cost–reward model   Piliavin *et al.*'s view that whether a bystander helps a victim depends on his or her level of arousal, and on the rewards and costs of different possible actions.

arousal level   Physiological term that describes how alert the BRAIN of a person or animal is to messages about the external world coming to it via the senses.

articulatory-phonological loop   The part of WORKING MEMORY that holds information for a short period of time in a phonological (sound) or speech-based form.

artificial intelligence (AI)   A sub-field of COGNITIVE SCIENCE that uses computer systems to develop machines that are intended to reproduce human thought processes.

asceticism   A way of life in which people deny themselves sensual pleasures in order to concentrate on what they consider to be a more important intellectual or spiritual life.

ascribed status   A sociological term for describing a position in society given to someone automatically because of something he or she has inherited at birth (like skin colour or family background). Contrasted with ACHIEVED STATUS.

assertiveness training   A technique of BEHAVIOUR MODIFICATION intended to help people overcome inhibitions about expressing their feelings without becoming aggressive. See ROLE PLAYING.

assimilation   In PIAGET's theory, dealing with new environmental situations by using existing cognitive organisation.

association   A learned connection between two ideas or events. One of psychology's oldest and most general concepts, it goes back at least as far as Aristotle in the fourth century BC. See LAWS OF ASSOCIATION.

association areas   Those parts of the CEREBRAL CORTEX that are involved in higher-order processing; such as associations between sensory and motor activity as well as language.

association test   See WORD ASSOCIATION TEST.

asylum   Literally, a place of refuge. An obsolete term for a mental institution.

atavistic   Genetic term for the reappearance of a trait that was not present in the most immediate ancestors of an organism. In psychology and the social sciences it is used to describe behaviour that is considered to be a throwback to a more primitive way of functioning.

attachment   This is a strong, reciprocal, emotional bond between an infant and his or her caregiver(s) that is characterised by a desire to maintain proximity. Attachments take different forms, such as secure or insecure. Infants display attachment through the degree of separation distress shown when separated from the caregiver, pleasure at reunion with the caregiver, and stranger anxiety. See also STRANGE SITUATION.

attention   The process of selecting one aspect of the complex sensory information from the environment to focus on, while disregarding others for the time being.

attitude   A stable, long-lasting, learned predisposition to respond to certain things in a certain way. The concept has a *cognitive* (belief) aspect, an *affective* (feeling) aspect, and a *conative* (intention) aspect. See COGNITION, AFFECT, and CONATION. (Figure 2.)

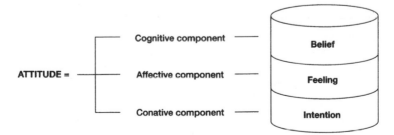

Figure 2   Attitude

11

attitude scale A set of questions designed to elicit attitudes and measure their strength.

attributions Statements about the causes of behaviour.

auditory cortex The part of the CEREBRAL CORTEX dedicated to hearing. It is located in the temporal lobes.

augmenting principle A heuristic for making ATTRIBUTIONS where explanations are selected if they appear to be "against the odds".

authoritarian personality An individual who holds rigid beliefs, hostility towards other groups, and submissive attitudes towards those in authority.

autistic Description of a child, possibly suffering from a neurological disorder, who is characterised by being withdrawn and unable to form relationships with people, to respond to environmental stimuli, or to use language. Adult thinking is sometimes described as autistic if it is guided by fantasy and wish-fulfilment rather than objective reality.

autokinetic effect A visual illusion where a small spot of light in a darkened room appears to be moving when in fact it is stationary.

automatic processes Processes that typically occur rapidly, do not require attention, and for which there is no conscious awareness.

autonomic conditioning CONDITIONING of involuntary functions controlled by the AUTONOMIC NERVOUS SYSTEM, such as digestion, heart rate, or salivation.

autonomic nervous system That part of the nervous system that controls vital body functions (like breathing and digestion), which is self-regulating and needs no conscious control (automatic).

autonomous morality A later stage of moral development, where the person's intentions are used as a basis for judgement. See HETERONOMOUS MORALITY.

autonomy stage The second of the eight stages of development through the human life cycle proposed by ERIK ERIKSON. This stage occurs between the ages of 1 or 1½ years and 3 or 3½ years. It is the time concerned with acquiring self-mastery and overcoming feels of doubt and shame. See EPIGENESIS and STAGE THEORY.

autosuggestion A suggestion coming from oneself with the object of attempting, consciously, to produce a change in one's behaviour.

availability heuristic   A mental shortcut based on how quickly instances come to mind.

aversion therapy   A form of treatment based on the principles of CLASSICAL CONDITIONING in which undesirable behaviour is eliminated by associating it with severe punishment, such as electric shocks.

avoidance   Tendency to withdraw from psychological conflict, often by substituting other, non-threatening activities.

avoidance–avoidance conflict   Caused by having to choose between two undesirable objects or goals.

avoidance learning   A form of OPERANT CONDITIONING where an animal learns to prevent an unpleasant or aversive situation by making a particular response to a stimulus. Usually the stimulus precedes the unpleasant situation.

avoidant attachment (type A)   An insecure attachment of an infant to its mother. The child avoids contact on reunion.

awareness   Knowing that you are experiencing something. Apart from strict behaviourists most psychologists would call this CONSCIOUSNESS.

B

babble   Speech sounds made by infants from which recognisable language develops.

Babinski reflex   Named after Joseph Babinski, a French neurologist, this is a normal reflex that occurs in infants below the age of 2 and then disappears. The toes curl upwards when the sole of the foot is stroked. If the Babinski reflex reappears in adulthood it is a sign of a disorder in the nervous system.

backward conditioning   The situation in which the unconditioned stimulus is presented just before the conditioned stimulus in CLASSICAL CONDITIONING.

balance theory   According to the American psychologist Fritz Heider people have a tendency towards compatibility in their beliefs because incompatibility causes tension. For example, if you believe someone is gentle and you see him acting violently your beliefs are in a state of imbalance. You would strive to balance them again and this might be done by saying that the act was not really violent, or the person was not as gentle as you thought, or he was not responsible for his behaviour. See COGNITIVE DISSONANCE.

bandwagon effect Social psychological term for the behaviour of people who feel a need to conform to the ATTITUDES or actions of a group they identify with. In the general parlance of social science the term is used to describe increasing support for a popular movement where more and more people want to "join the bandwagon".

barbiturates Drugs that used to be widely used in the treatment of ANXIETY disorders.

bar chart Like a HISTOGRAM, a representation of frequency data but the categories do not have to be continuous; used for nominal data.

Bard–Cannon theory A neurological theory of emotion which proposes that stimuli from the environment trigger off responses in the HYPOTHALAMUS which alert both the BRAIN and the AUTONOMIC NERVOUS SYSTEM. The key point of this theory, in contrast to the JAMES–LANGE THEORY, is that the feelings associated with emotion come from the hypothalamus and these feelings are experienced first before we recognise them cognitively. So, for example we cry *because* we are sad.

basal ganglia A group of subcortical structures (most importantly the caudate nucleus, the putamen, and the globus pallidus) with extensive interconnections with other areas of the BRAIN. Involved in movement, language and emotion.

basic mistrust According to ERIK ERIKSON the pain of being thrust out of the all-supporting womb and into the harsh external world produces a state of basic mistrust in ourselves and in the world. Our first developmental task is therefore to acquire a sense of BASIC TRUST.

basic personality A concept proposed by the American social anthropologist Abraham Kardiner that the patterns of personality characteristics will be similar for most people of a given society because of their similar childhood experiences, and they would therefore share unconsciously held unquestioned assumptions about life.

basic trust According to ERIK ERIKSON the acquisition of a sense of basic trust in oneself and in the world is the major task to be accomplished during the first 12 to 18 months of life. Basic trust is acquired if the infant's physical needs are met, if normal biological maturation occurs, and, most important, if the infant is loved and cared for by a mother who is herself trusting and self-confident. See also STAGE THEORY.

battle fatigue   A state of psychological disorder, sometimes taking the form of a CONVERSION HYSTERIA, resulting from the exhaustion, STRESS, and ANXIETY of warfare. It can usually be cured after the patient is removed from the scene of the battle.

Bayley Scales of Infant Development   A well-known American test for assessing the development of infants and young children.

becoming   A key concept of EXISTENTIAL PSYCHOLOGY. It describes the process of individual development leading towards the goal of being as human as possible, fulfilling as much of one's potential as possible, and being at one with the world. See also LAING.

Bedlam   Probably a corruption of St Mary of Bethlehem, a hospital for mental patients founded in London in the 16th century. Because of this association the name has been popularly used for any place in a noisy, chaotic state, or any condition of wild disorder.

behaviour modification   The deliberate changing of a particular pattern of behaviour by behaviourist methods. See AVERSION THERAPY and OPERANT CONDITIONING.

behaviour therapy   A form of therapy based on the assumptions of BEHAVIOURISM and using behaviourist means to eliminate undesirable behaviour and to encourage desirable or appropriate responses. See also AVERSION THERAPY. Compare with CLIENT-CENTRED THERAPY and PSYCHOANALYSIS.

behavioural genetics   The study of the effects of GENES on the expression of behaviour. See PHENOTYPE. It includes both the study of genetic abnormalities and the all-encompassing NATURE–NURTURE DEBATE.

behavioural model of abnormality   A model of abnormality that considers individuals who suffer from mental disorders possess maladaptive forms of behaviour, which have been learned. Now often includes SOCIAL LEARNING THEORY.

behavioural science   The study of the behaviour of humans and animals by experiment and observation. Centred around psychology but branching out into biology and physiology on the one hand, anthropology and sociology on the other (Figure 3).

behavioural therapy   Forms of clinical therapy based on the

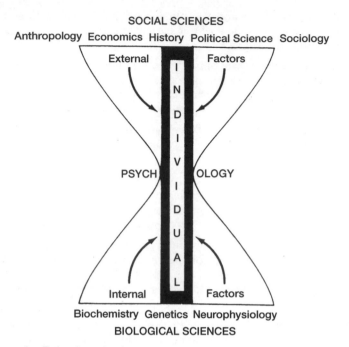

SOCIAL SCIENCES
Anthropology Economics History Political Science Sociology

External | Factors

I
N
D
I
V
PSYCH | OLOGY
I
D
U
A
L

Internal | Factors

Biochemistry Genetics Neurophysiology
BIOLOGICAL SCIENCES

Figure 3 Behavioural science

learning principles associated with CLASSICAL and OPERANT CONDITIONING.

Behaviourism An approach to psychology based on learning theory that focuses only on observable behaviour and rejects any reference to internal mental activity. Founded in the United States by J. B. WATSON and developed by B. F. SKINNER.

belief system A set of mutually supportive beliefs held by an individual or group.

bell-shaped curve Describes the shape of the curve obtained by plotting the frequency of a NORMAL DISTRIBUTION.

Bender-Gestalt Test A test for BRAIN DAMAGE that requires the subject to copy some simple designs.

benzodiazepines Anti-anxiety drugs such as Valium and Librium. They work by reducing serotonin levels and are generally considered more effective in reducing the experience of ANXIETY than BARBITURATES.

Bernreuter Personality Inventory One of the earliest

PAPER-AND-PENCIL TESTS of PERSONALITY (dating from the 1930s), which attempted to tease out the different aspects of the term with scales of introversion, confidence, etc.

beta bias   The tendency to minimise differences between the sexes.

beta rhythm   BRAIN WAVES associated with mental activity rather than with resting. They appear as shallower and more frequent waves than those of the ALPHA RHYTHM.

biased sample   Term used in social surveys or any area where a conclusion is to be made about a large population. The sample of the population being studied is considered biased if it is unrepresentative of the population as a whole, e.g., if you say something about national opinion on a certain topic after interviewing your friends.

bilateral   When behavioural functions are equally represented in both CEREBRAL HEMISPHERES.

bilateral transfer   Transferring a skill learned on one side of the body to the other side. For example right-footed people learning to kick with their left feet. See LATERALITY.

bimodal distribution   A FREQUENCY DISTRIBUTION that has two MODES.

Binet, Alfred (1857–1911)   A French psychologist who was asked by the Paris school system to find some way of predicting which children would not do well in school (and thus by implication those who would). To accomplish this task he invented and standardised the first example of what came to be called an INTELLIGENCE TEST. See also BINET SCALE and STANFORD–BINET.

Binet Scale   A series of items invented by ALFRED BINET for predicting a child's performance in school. The items were arranged in order of difficulty and standardised by age. See also STANFORD–BINET.

binocular cues   Visual cues about depth provided by information from both eyes.

binocular disparity   The difference in the image of any given object on the two retinas. See DEPTH PERCEPTION and VISUAL CLIFF.

binocular fusion   The way the brain fuses the different images from each of our eyes into one visual perception so that we are quite unaware of the BINOCULAR DISPARITY.

biofeedback   A technique that aims to control involuntary (autonomic) muscles through the use of FEEDBACK about current physiological functioning. Relaxation is an important aspect of its success when used in the context of STRESS.

biological clock   A biological pacemaker that governs rhythms such as the sleep–wake cycle. In humans this function is located in the SUPRACHIASMATIC NUCLEUS.

biological determinism   The view that behaviour is determined by internal biological systems, e.g., physiological or genetic mechanisms.

biosocial   The interaction of biological and social factors in the study of society, e.g., the social effects of decreased birth rate or bubonic plague.

bipolar disorder   A disorder in which a person's mood swings between the opposite poles of MANIA and DEPRESSION. A more modern way of describing the traditional categorisation, MANIC-DEPRESSIVE.

birth order   The order of birth of the children in a family. Psychologists have long been interested in the possible connections between birth order and PERSONALITY traits but so far the evidence is slight. See NEED FOR AFFILIATION.

birth trauma   The shock of the sudden transition from the security and comfort of the womb to the harsh insecurity of the outside world. Some psychoanalysts believe this to be the source of adult ANXIETY and something that must be dealt with before a person can become psychologically mature and free of NEUROSIS. See also BASIC MISTRUST.

bisexuality   Possessing the physical or psychological characteristics of both sexes. Also used now to mean sexual responsiveness to both men and women.

black box   Used in scientific theorising to indicate something that seems to work, though nobody knows how it works or what goes on inside the "box". It is often used as an analogy for the BRAIN, or in a more general sense for any experiment in psychology where the input is controlled, the output is observed, and an inference made from the one to the other to account for what has happened in between.

Blacky pictures   A PROJECTIVE TECHNIQUE for disturbed children, using cartoons about a family of dogs (with a central character called Blacky). The cartoons portray relationships found in human families. The child is asked to make up stories about the cartoons and these are scanned for evidence of emotional problems.

blaming the victim   See JUST-WORLD HYPOTHESIS.

Bleuler, Eugen (1857–1939) Swiss PSYCHIATRIST and early follower of FREUD. He invented the term SCHIZOPHRENIA.

blind spot The area of the RETINA where the OPTIC NERVE leaves the eye. This area is insensitive to light and the eye is therefore "blind" at that point. Also used now to refer to an area of someone's (otherwise rational) beliefs that is impervious to change through objective information or rational argument.

blindsight A phenomenon in which BRAIN-DAMAGED patients can perform simple visual tasks even though they have no conscious awareness of seeing.

blob The central portion of a module within the primary VISUAL CORTEX that responds strongly to contrast and colour.

blocking The failure of a conditioned stimulus to produce a conditioned response because another conditioned stimulus already predicts the presentation of the unconditioned stimulus.

body image The picture a person has of how his or her body appears to other people. This image develops early in life and because of bodily changes it may in later life be markedly inaccurate. Body image is at the root of one's SELF-IMAGE.

body language NON-VERBAL COMMUNICATION with other people by means of physical postures, movements, or gestures that may be conscious or UNCONSCIOUS.

bond disruption When a child is deprived of their main ATTACHMENT object, in the short or long term, and receives no substitute emotional care.

bonding The process of forming close ties with another. See BOWLBY.

boomerang effect A term used in SOCIAL PSYCHOLOGY in the study of ATTITUDE change. It refers to someone who changes their attitude in the opposite direction from that being advocated.

borderline (1) When used of mental ability it is usually defined as an IQ score between 70 and 80. (2) In CLINICAL PSYCHOLOGY it is sometimes used to describe someone whose emotional disturbance appears to be more severe than NEUROSIS but is not quite PSYCHOSIS.

bottom-up processing Gathering information directly from the external environment, as distinct from the effects of expectations (TOP-DOWN PROCESSING).

Bowlby, John (1907–1990) British psychiatrist who pioneered the study of BONDING between mother and infant and the effects of MATERNAL DEPRIVATION on young infants.

brain The part of the CENTRAL NERVOUS SYSTEM contained within the skull. It is the most complex and least understood part of the human body. Because of the brain's organising role in all human behaviour it is sometimes compared to a central computer that stores, retrieves, and utilises information. But the brain is infinitely more complex and powerful than that. In an important sense our brain is what makes us human. All the limitless forms of human behaviour are a direct result of the brain's capacity. (Figure 4.)

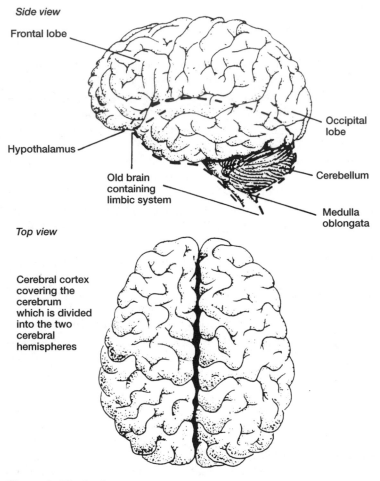

Side view

Frontal lobe

Occipital lobe

Hypothalamus

Old brain containing limbic system

Cerebellum

Medulla oblongata

Top view

Cerebral cortex covering the cerebrum which is divided into the two cerebral hemispheres

Figure 4 The brain

brain damage   Any physical injury to the brain whether by accident, disease, drugs, or surgery; usually results in impairment of behaviour and emotional disturbance.

brain localisation   The controversial hypothesis that specific mental experiences or functions are associated with specific areas of the brain.

brain potential   In brain physiology, the level of electrical activity in the brain.

brain stimulation   The electrical stimulation of certain parts of the brain in order to study their functions.

brainstorming   In SOCIAL PSYCHOLOGY this is the free generation of ideas by the members of a group for the purpose of solving a specific problem.

brainwashing   An attempt to coerce someone into radically changing their beliefs or behaviour by using physical, psychological, or social pressures.

brain waves   The recorded rhythms of the electrical activity of the brain (Figure 5).

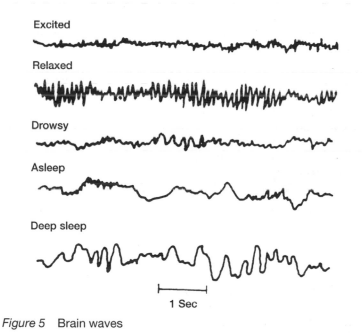

Figure 5   Brain waves

breakthrough   Used in PSYCHOTHERAPY to describe a patient's sudden INSIGHT about a problem after overcoming his or her resistance to dealing with it. See also ABREACTION and AHA REACTION.

brightness constancy   The experience of perceiving an object as maintaining the same level of brightness even though the objective illumination seen by the eye may change.

Broca's Area   Named after Paul Broca, a 19th-century French surgeon, it is an area of the BRAIN closely involved with producing speech and formerly referred to as the speech centre. It is situated in the left CEREBRAL HEMISPHERE of all right-handed people (i.e., over 90% of the population), although not in many left-handed people. Compare with WERNICKE'S AREA.

brood parasitism   When a parent animal rears offspring of another animal placed in the nest, as it if it were their own (cuckoos are the best-known example).

buffers   Term used to refer to aspects of situations that protect people from having to confront the results of their actions.

bulimia nervosa   An eating disorder in which excessive (binge) eating is followed by compensatory behaviour such as self-induced vomiting or misuse of laxatives. It is often experienced as an unbreakable cycle where the bulimic impulsively overeats and then has to purge to reduce ANXIETY and feelings of GUILT about the amount of food consumed, which can add up to thousands of calories at a time. This disorder is not associated with excessive weight loss.

burnout   Physical and/or emotional exhaustion produced especially by STRESS.

bystander apathy   Refers to the tendency of people in a social situation not to go to the aid of strangers in an emergency. Apparently the more bystanders there are the greater may be the apathy because responsibility is then perceived as more diffuse and not vested in any one individual.

C

CA   Chronological age. Used along with MENTAL AGE in computing an IQ score.

CAI   See COMPUTER ASSISTED INSTRUCTION.

California F-Scale   See F-SCALE.

California Infant Scale   Now more commonly referred to as the BAYLEY SCALES OF INFANT DEVELOPMENT.

Cannon–Bard theory   See BARD-CANNON THEORY.

capacity   A measurement of how much can be held in either short-term or long-term memory.

cardiovascular disorders   These are disorders of the cardio-vascular system, which includes the heart and its supporting systems. An example is atherosclerosis, which is thickening inside the arteries due to high levels of cholesterol in the bloodstream. Another disorder is hypertension or high blood pressure, which puts pressure on the heart as it has to work harder to beat at high pressure.

caregiving sensitivity hypothesis   Secure ATTACHMENTS are due to a caregiver's sensitivity and responsiveness, which creates independence in the infant.

castration complex   According to FREUD, a COMPLEX caused in men by unconscious fears of losing their penis, and in women by the fantasy of once having had a penis and then losing it. This complex supposedly has a universal origin in childhood anxiety about being castrated as a punishment for harbouring sexual desire. See also PENIS ENVY.

CAT   See CHILDREN'S APPERCEPTION TEST.

catalepsy   A state of muscular rigidity associated with severe psychological disturbance, or a hypnotic trance, where a person whose body or limbs are placed in a certain position will maintain that position for a long period of time.

cataplexy   Immobility caused by fear or shock. Not to be confused with CATALEPSY.

catatonic   Descriptive of psychotic state generally considered to be a form of SCHIZOPHRENIA. Characterised by violent changes in behaviour from mainly rigid, frozen states (including CATALEPSY) to occasional extremes of excitement and activity.

categorical differentiation   Exaggerating the differences between two social categories in order to simplify and to organise our social worlds.

catharsis   Ancient Greek term for the purging of emotions by seeing them enacted on the stage. In PSYCHOTHERAPY (particularly PSYCHOANALYSIS) it is used generally to describe the release of emotional tension when a conflict is overcome or an insight achieved (see ABREACTION). It is used in literature to describe emotional relief in general.

cathexis   Used mainly in PSYCHOANALYSIS to refer to the psychic energy a patient invests in a person, place, idea, or thing. Emotions associated with the object of cathexis may be keenly aroused whenever it is re-encountered.

CAT scan   A three-dimensional picture of a cross-section of the brain produced with the use of X-rays; in this case, CAT stands for computerised axial tomography.

cautious shift   A form of GROUP POLARISATION where people make more cautious decisions under the influence of a group than by themselves. The opposite of RISKY SHIFT.

censorship   In PSYCHOANALYSIS, the regulation of the repressed material in the UNCONSCIOUS to see that nothing threatening to the EGO is allowed to escape into CONSCIOUSNESS. Censorship is apparently relaxed during sleep when repressed material is expressed in the form of dreams.

central executive   The key component of WORKING MEMORY. It is a modality-free system (i.e., not visual or auditory) of limited capacity and similar to "paying attention" to something.

central nervous system   Part of the nervous system that consists of the BRAIN and the spinal cord.

central organising trait   According to the American psychologist Gordon Allport, a TRAIT that is characteristic of an individual's PERSONALITY and associated with many other traits. For example the descriptions "warm" or "cold" are thought to be key terms.

central tendency   See MEASURES OF CENTRAL TENDENCY

centration   Attending to only one aspect of a situation.

centring   In GESTALT PSYCHOLOGY, the perfect integration of an organism and its environment.

cephalocaudal   Literally, "head-tail". Usually refers to the process of maturation in humans and animals where the sequence of physical development proceeds from the head downwards. Compare with PROXIMODISTAL.

cerebellum   Part of the BRAIN, at the back near the top of the spinal cord. It is thought to be involved in maintaining muscle tone and coordinating movement and balance.

cerebral cortex   The surface layer of the forebrain or CEREBRUM, made up mainly of NEURONS.

cerebral dominance The tendency for one CEREBRAL HEMI-SPHERE or the other to be dominant in its regulation of behaviour—the left hemisphere in right-handed people, the right in left-handed people.

cerebral hemispheres The two symmetrical left and right halves of the CEREBRUM. The right hemisphere controls the left side of the body, the left hemisphere the right side. See SPLIT-BRAIN PATIENTS.

cerebrum The main division of the brain in all vertebrates but much more highly developed in humans than in any other. It is thought to be crucially involved in processing sensory information and in all forms of cognitive activity. See COGNITION.

cff See CRITICAL FLICKER FREQUENCY.

change agent A term that is sometimes used by people who try to apply SOCIAL PSYCHOLOGY to social situations. It refers to someone whose task is to stimulate social change in what is considered a desirable direction. For example, raising the consciousness of an exploited group to the point of understanding and attempting to remove the exploitation.

character armour A concept, suggested by the psychoanalyst Wilhelm Reich, that to protect the ego an individual can put up a powerful front which dominates their whole PERSONALITY. For example, disguising hatred as love in dealing with a spouse or parent. Reich regarded the piercing of this armour as a key task for PSYCHOANALYSIS. See also REACTION FORMATION.

character disorder A behaviour disorder characterised by immaturity and a general inability to cope with adult life. It often takes the form of social problems like alcoholism, drug addiction, or criminal behaviour. Some psychologists would place an ANTI-SOCIAL PERSONALITY in this category.

Charcot, Jean Marie (1825–1893) French physician and early PSYCHOTHERAPIST whose use of HYPNOSIS to reach the depth of his patients' problems led him to the conclusion that all NEUROSIS had sexual roots. However he bowed to his Victorian ethos and never made this conclusion public. One of his students, SIGMUND FREUD, as well as adopting his teacher's methods and conclusions, did have the courage of his convictions and made his beliefs public. Freud was, however, sufficiently impressed by Charcot to name one of his children after him.

charisma From the Greek word for "gift" and used originally for the "gift of divine grace". An elusive quality of PERSONALITY often defined as "personal magnetism", which is considered by some social scientists to be an essential element in LEADERSHIP while others consider it to be largely manufactured.

child development   The study of the growing child physiologically, mentally, emotionally and socially. The most important aspect of DEVELOPMENTAL PSYCHOLOGY.

childhood   Usually defined as the period of human development between birth (or sometimes infancy) and puberty, at around 12 years of age, i.e., a biological definition. Marking this period off from every other, treating people differently during it, and expecting different behaviour from them, gives it a particular psychological importance. In this sense childhood is not a universal phenomenon. It varies culturally and historically and in some societies does not even appear to exist. See AGEISM.

childhood amnesia   See INFANTILE AMNESIA.

Children's Apperception Test (CAT)   A version of the THEMATIC APPERCEPTION TEST adapted for children.

child's theory of mind   A phrase sometimes used to describe the mental processes by which children make sense of the world as they change and develop. See COGNITIVE DEVELOPMENT.

chi-squared test   A statistical test of association that is used with nominal data in the form of frequencies.

choice shift   American term for GROUP POLARISATION.

chromosomes   The parts of a cell nucleus that carry the GENES.

chronobiology   The study of the BIOLOGICAL CLOCK.

chunking   The process of combining items of information, like letters or numbers, into larger, meaningful units as an aid to memorising them.

cingulotomy   A form of PSYCHOSURGERY where the cingulate gyrus is destroyed using strong electrical currents to reduce aggressive behaviour.

circadian rhythm   A biological rhythm that recurs approximately every 24 hours; "*circa*" and "*dies*" mean "around the day". The most obvious example is the sleep–wake cycle.

circannual rhythm   A biological rhythm that recurs approximately once a year, such as annual migration.

clairvoyance   The ability to see or perceive things without the use of the eyes or other sense organs, i.e., a form of EXTRASENSORY PERCEPTION. See also PARAPSYCHOLOGY.

classical conditioning A basic form of learning in which simple responses are associated with new stimuli. First demonstrated experimentally by IVAN PAVLOV.

claustrophobia PHOBIA of confined spaces.

Clever Hans Name of a German horse reputed to have advanced skills in arithmetic. In fact Hans was responding (cleverly) to very subtle and unconscious cues from his trainer about when to start "counting" by pawing the ground, and when to stop. Clever Hans is symptomatic of the ANTHROPOMORPHISM that has plagued the study of psychology since people first began to domesticate animals and were struck by some of their apparently human responses. This phenomenon became more complex with the attention paid to the role of language in thought. Some psychologists have been struck by the apparently human linguistic abilities of chimps. Although this claim is harder to disprove than the case of Clever Hans, there is no clear evidence that chimps, or any other animals, have the linguistic and intellectual understanding or creativity of humans. See also EXPERIMENTER BIAS, ROSENTHAL EFFECT and SELF-FULFILLING PROPHECY for other examples of the same kind of phenomenon.

client Used of someone who seeks counselling or PSYCHOTHERAPY from a practitioner with a HUMANISTIC or non-directive approach.

client-centred therapy A form of HUMANISTIC therapy introduced by CARL ROGERS and designed to increase the client's SELF-ESTEEM.

clinical method A form of unstructured INTERVIEW where the interviewer starts with some predetermined set of questions, but as the interview proceeds these questions are adapted in line with the responses given. This kind of interview is used by clinicians when assessing mentally ill patients.

clinical psychologist A practitioner of CLINICAL PSYCHOLOGY, usually with a PhD in the subject. Clinical psychologists may also be PSYCHOANALYSTS or other kinds of PSYCHOTHERAPISTS. They may work in hospitals or clinics or they may have a private practice. Compare with PSYCHIATRIST.

clinical psychology The branch of psychology concerned with the application of psychological theory and research to the diagnosis and treatment of emotional, mental, or behavioural disorders. Compare with PSYCHIATRY.

clock shifting This involves changing an animal's internal daily rhythms relative to external time.

closure A principle of GESTALT PSYCHOLOGY that has generally been accepted in the study of PERCEPTION, i.e., that the brain has a built-in tendency to perceive meaning, completion, and coherence where the objective sensory facts may have no meaning, be incomplete, or incoherent. Thus a figure with a part missing will be perceived as though it were whole (Figure 6). The term is also used

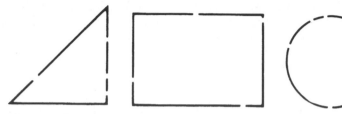

Figure 6 Closure

in PSYCHOTHERAPY (and even in general parlance) to denote a line of investigation that has been opened up and completed.

clustering See CHUNKING.

CNS See CENTRAL NERVOUS SYSTEM.

coacting group Sociological term for people who share the same goal but work towards it without communicating or interacting.

cocktail party effect The ability to be aware of the physical characteristics of a non-attended message when focused on another message or conversation and "tuning out" all other noise.

coefficient of relatedness The probability that an ALLELE chosen at random from one individual will also be present in another individual.

co-evolution Where two forms of behaviour, such as that of prey and predator, evolve in unison because changes in one behaviour act as a form of SELECTIVE PRESSURE on the other.

cognition A general term that includes all the mental processes by which people become aware of, and gain knowledge about, the world.

cognitive-behavioural therapy A development of COGNITIVE THERAPY where some elements of BEHAVIOURAL THERAPY (such as a focus on behaviour change) have been added.

cognitive bias A predisposition to think in a certain way.

cognitive development The development of the child's mental processes such as thought, reasoning, and memory. IQ tests and the child's academic performance at school are used to assess cognitive development. Cognitive development is determined by an interaction of biological predisposition and the environment.

cognitive dissonance A kind of BALANCE THEORY proposed by the American psychologist Leon Festinger; the theory states that because we have a powerful DRIVE towards consistency (or consonance), if we hold two psychologically inconsistent cognitions (beliefs, attitudes, values, or ideas) at the same time, or if our behaviour clashes with those cognitions, we will be in an unpleasant state of tension which we are strongly motivated to reduce. As the theory deals with *psychological* rather than logical inconsistency, it proposes that we are not so much concerned with actually being consistent as with feeling that we are consistent.

cognitive ergonomics That aspect of ERGONOMICS which deals with the interaction between people and the computer-based information technology they work with.

cognitive labelling theory A theory of EMOTION proposing that all emotional experiences are preceded by a generalised state of physiological arousal which is then "labelled" on the basis of situational cues and past experience.

cognitive learning theory A school of thought in PSYCHOLOGY that opposed the behaviourist view that there is a direct link between stimulus and response via the nervous system, arguing that complex learning involves the restructuring and reorganising of knowledge and ideas by the BRAIN. Contrast with BEHAVIOURISM.

cognitive map A mental representation of spatial relationships in an animal's immediate environment.

cognitive model of abnormality A model of ABNORMALITY that emphasises the role of cognitive factors in mental disorders. The view is that thinking in a maladaptive way leads to disordered behaviour.

cognitive neuropsychology An area of research concerned with trying to understand the workings of the cognitive system by studying brain-damaged patients and the kinds of impairment associated with BRAIN DAMAGE.

cognitive neuroscience Using various techniques for the study of BRAIN functioning (e.g., brain scans) to understand human COGNITION.

cognitive overload A situation in which someone is receiving more information than he or she can process.

cognitive priming The idea that cues, e.g., violent TV programmes, lead to thoughts and feelings that produce aggression.

cognitive psychology The branch of psychology that deals with COGNITION, particularly the processes of PERCEPTION, LEARNING, language, MEMORY and thinking.

cognitive restructuring The technique used by cognitive therapists to make distorted and irrational beliefs more rational.

cognitive revolution A phrase used to describe a great upsurge of research, theorising, and applications using a COGNITIVE PSYCHOLOGY perspective, beginning in the 1970s and especially prominent in European psychology. This was part of a broader movement in COGNITIVE SCIENCE stimulated by developments in ARTIFICIAL INTELLIGENCE and information technology that led to an increasing sophistication in the study of mind.

cognitive science The term now used for the group of disciplines that study the mind, including ARTIFICIAL INTELLIGENCE, COGNITIVE NEUROSCIENCE and COGNITIVE PSYCHOLOGY.

cognitive therapy A form of treatment involving attempts to change or restructure the client's thoughts and beliefs on the assumption that they exert great influence on his or her EMOTIONS and behaviour. Pioneered as RATIONAL-EMOTIVE THERAPY by Albert Ellis. An emphasis on dealing with the person's "cognitive distortions" has also been used by followers of Aaron Beck to treat common disorders like ANXIETY and DEPRESSION.

cognitive triad Negative thoughts about the self, the world, and the future, found in depressed clients. See also DEPRESSION.

cohort effect When a group of individuals of similar age (a cohort) is unique because of historical events during development, such as those people who were children in the 1940s. If research is conducted with this group the results may not generalise to other groups due to the cohort effect.

cold emotion A psychological state resulting from the injection of ADRENALINE. The bodily changes that occur resemble those associated with an emotional experience, but the subjects report feeling that they should be having an emotional experience without actually doing so, i.e., they feel tense or excited without knowing why.

collective mind (1) The idea that there are mental attributes of a group over and above those of the individuals composing it. (2) The idea that a group shares common mental processes that lead it to take concerted action.

collectivist When used of a CULTURE, one where individuals share tasks, belongings, and income. The people in a collectivist culture may live in large family groups and value interdependence. Contrast with INDIVIDUALISTIC.

colour blindness A total or partial inability to distinguish colours. Total colour blindness is very rare but partial colour blindness (particularly the inability to distinguish red and green from each other or from grey) is surprisingly common. It has been estimated that about 8–10% of males are born with this defect, although it is rare in women.

colour constancy The tendency for an object to be perceived as having the same colour under varying viewing conditions.

colour contrast The tendency for the difference between two colours to be intensified when they are placed side by side.

colour vision The process by which the eye discriminates between different wave lengths of light, thus providing the BRAIN with the information necessary to perceive what we describe as colours.

combat fatigue See BATTLE FATIGUE.

communicator credibility In SOCIAL PSYCHOLOGY the extent to which the communicator of a message is believable. Thought to be related to whether the communicator is perceived as expert and trustworthy or not.

community psychology A combination of applied CLINICAL and SOCIAL PSYCHOLOGY that attempts to foster the well-being of psychologically disturbed people by intervening in their social environment and utilising the resources of their community to help them adapt.

comorbidity The presence of two or more disorders in a given individual at the same time.

comparative psychology The branch of psychology that compares different species, including humans, and attempts to understand the similarities and differences in their mental and behavioural lives.

comparison level The outcomes that people think they deserve from a relationship on the basis of past experience.

compensation As used in PSYCHOANALYSIS this is a DEFENCE MECHANISM in which a person perceives himself or herself to be lacking in some way and tries to make up for it by substituting some other characteristic which is perhaps exaggerated. This was a key concept in the work of ALFRED ADLER who suggested that, in this way, a

31

small man might compensate for his lack of size by being aggressive and dominating psychologically. See INFERIORITY COMPLEX.

completion test   Name given to a mental test that requires the subject to fill in the missing letter, word or phrase. First devised by the German psychologist Hermann von Ebbinghaus in the late 19th century.

complex   In PSYCHOANALYSIS, a group of repressed emotionally charged ideas that conflict with other ideas (representing other aspects of the PERSONALITY) that the individual is conscious of.

compliance   Conforming to the majority view in order to be liked, or to avoid ridicule, or social exclusion. Compliance occurs more readily with public behaviour than private behaviour, and is based on power.

compulsion   An overwhelming UNCONSCIOUS need to engage in some behaviour that is usually contrary to one's conscious wishes. Compare with OBSESSION.

computer-assisted instruction (CAI)   A method of PROGRAMMED LEARNING in which a computer is used as a teaching machine.

conation   A vague term used to denote a general psychological activity variously described as impulse, desire, will, and striving. Sometimes used along with AFFECT and COGNITION as a tripartite division of psychological life.

concept formation   A particularly human form of mental ability that seems to be closely associated with the use of language. It involves the BRAIN in abstracting the essential qualities of individual things and classifying them by higher-order rules or groups.

concordance rate   If one twin has a disorder or condition, the likelihood that the other twin also has it.

concrete operations stage   The third stage in PIAGET's theory of COGNITIVE DEVELOPMENT, from 7 to 11 years. The child can now use adult internally consistent logic but only when the problem is presented in a concrete way.

concrete thinking   Thinking that is rigidly confined to the experiences of the moment. Often due to BRAIN DAMAGE. Sometimes used in the more general sense of thinking in concrete rather than abstract terms because it is easier, or being unable to see the forest for the trees.

conditioned response   A response resulting solely from the process of conditioning. See also CLASSICAL CONDITIONING and PAVLOV.

conditioned stimulus   A stimulus that is originally ineffective in eliciting a given response but becomes effective after a process of conditioning. See also CLASSICAL CONDITIONING and PAVLOV.

conditioning A process of learning in humans or animals, via an experimental procedure, where a given stimulus produces a response other than its normal, natural, or automatic one. In CLASSICAL CONDITIONING developed by PAVLOV a dog learned to salivate at the sound of a bell or buzzer and not just at the presentation of food. Later B. F. SKINNER developed a different procedure known as OPERANT CONDITIONING in which an animal's simple response could be used as the basis for training it to engage in very complex behaviour.

conditioning theory The view that all behaviour can be explained in terms of stimulus–response links.

conduction aphasia In this condition, patients can understand speech and speak fluently and meaningfully, but cannot repeat non-words or unfamiliar words; produced by damage to the ARCUATE FASCICULUS.

cones Photoreceptors in the RETINA that are specialised for COLOUR VISION and sharpness of vision.

confabulation Filling in blanks in the MEMORY with plausible stories that are untrue but not deliberate lies. Occurs in people whose memory is disturbed through BRAIN DAMAGE and who don't realise that their stories are confabulations.

confirmation bias A preference for information that supports rather than disproves our predictions.

conformity/majority influence This occurs when people adopt the behaviour, attitudes, or values of the majority (dominant or largest group) after being exposed to their values or behaviour. In this sense they publicly yield to group pressure (COMPLIANCE), although in some cases they yield privately (INTERNALISATION). The majority is able to exert influence because of other people's desire to be accepted (NORMATIVE SOCIAL INFLUENCE) or their desire to be right (INFORMATIONAL SOCIAL INFLUENCE).

confounding variables Variables that are mistakenly manipulated or allowed to vary along with the INDEPENDENT VARIABLE and therefore affect the DEPENDENT VARIABLE.

congenital Something that is present in an individual at birth but is not necessarily genetically inherited, or INNATE.

connectionism A theory of COGNITIVE SCIENCE opposed to the older INFORMATION PROCESSING model as a way of understanding mental functioning. It suggests the BRAIN operates as a network, capable of performing many operations at the same time and also of learning from its experience, unlike a computer which operates sequentially (i.e., a form of *processing* in which the operations are *distributed* over a vast network and occur in *parallel*.)

consciousness   The awareness of oneself in every aspect of one's being.

consensual validation   Checking one's PERCEPTION of something with other people as a way of knowing whether what is perceived is real or illusory.

conserve (conservation)   To understand that quantity does not change even when a display is transformed, i.e., the quantity is conserved.

consolidation   The idea that after something has been learned physiological changes take place in the BRAIN that help fix it in the MEMORY.

conspecifics   Members of the same species.

constant object of love   According to the American PSYCHO-ANALYST Margaret Mahler, a form of emotional OBJECT CONSTANCY where the mother is perceived as the constant object of love.

construct validity   See VALIDITY.

consumer psychology   The study of people as buyers and con-sumers of goods and services. It started in the 1960s mainly with a PSYCHOANALYTIC interpretation of product choice. More recently COGNITIVE and SOCIAL approaches have become very influential, especially in studying the effects of advertising and marketing.

contact hypothesis   The notion that mere contact between groups can reduce prejudice. See EQUAL-STATUS CONTACT.

contagion theory of crowds   A modern variant in sociology of the old idea of GROUP MIND. In this version the effect of a crowd is to assimilate individuals within it, producing an overriding psycho-logical unity and changing an individual's usual psychological responses in the process. Compare with COLLECTIVE MIND.

contamination   In EXPERIMENTAL PSYCHOLOGY, the distorting effect of uncontrolled facts external to the experiment, the most important being the conscious or unconscious assumptions of the experimenter. See EXPERIMENTER BIAS and ROSENTHAL EFFECT.

content analysis   The analysis of material in PSYCHOLOGY and in SOCIAL SCIENCE to see what categories or themes emerge, or the analysis of material by prearranged themes or categories to test a HYPOTHESIS or make a diagnosis.

context-dependent learning RECALL is better when it occurs in the same context as original LEARNING. May result in learning that some behaviours are appropriate in some contexts and not in others.

contiguity One of the LAWS OF ASSOCIATION first introduced in the fourth century BC by Aristotle. The idea that the BRAIN tends to associate stimuli that occur close together in time or space (Figure 7).

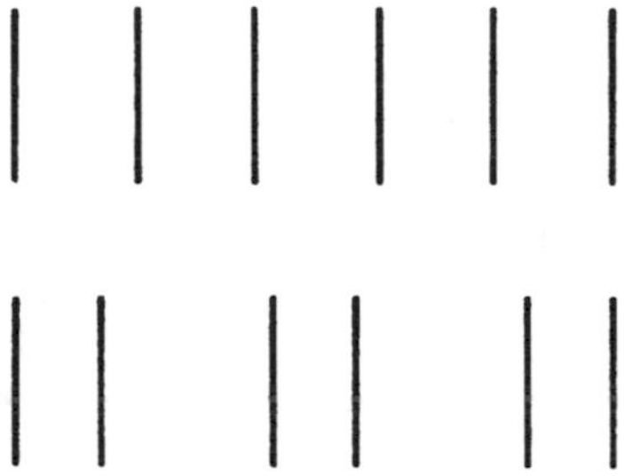

Figure 7 Contiguity. We see six single lines on top, but three pairs of lines below.

continuity Similar to CONTIGUITY and associated with GESTALT PSYCHOLOGY. The idea that the BRAIN will perceive stimuli as belonging with each other and forming a pattern if they follow each other closely and regularly in time or space.

continuous reinforcement Schedule of OPERANT CONDITIONING when REINFORCEMENT is given after every response (as opposed to various forms of partial reinforcement).

contour The outline or boundary of an object, which is essential to its PERCEPTION.

contralateral When behavioural functions on one side of the body are controlled by the opposite CEREBRAL HEMISPHERE.

control This refers to the PERCEPTION of being in command (control) of one's responses to stimuli, such as STRESSORS. Self-perception is the crux of this, as according to the transactional model, a lack of control and consequently STRESS may be experienced when there is a mismatch between the perceived demands of the situation and the individual's perceived ability to cope. Perception of control gives the individual a sense of SELF-EFFICACY, that is, they perceive that they can cope with the stressor.

control group In EXPERIMENTAL PSYCHOLOGY, a group of subjects as similar as possible to the EXPERIMENTAL GROUP for purposes of comparison. They share the same conditions as the experimental group except exposure to the EXPERIMENTAL VARIABLE which is the object of the study.

conventional stage According to the American psychologist Lawrence Kohlberg, the second of three broad levels of MORAL DEVELOPMENT—beyond which most people do not mature. At this level people judge the rightness or wrongness of an action in terms of what other people think and the dictates of authority. See STAGE THEORY.

convergent thinking Thinking along conventional lines in an attempt to find the best single answer to a problem. Compare with DIVERGENT THINKING.

conversion hysteria The kind of HYSTERIA, especially common in the early days of PSYCHOANALYSIS, that converts psychological conflict into the form of serious physical problems like paralysis. Such striking phenomena are now rare, apart from BATTLE FATIGUE, (perhaps because of increased sophistication about UNCONSCIOUS dynamics), although SOMATISING and PSYCHOSOMATIC illnesses are still with us.

core sleep Those aspects of sleep that are more essential to survival. See also DREAM SLEEP.

cornea A transparent membrane at the front of the eye.

corpus callosum A bundle of nerve fibres that connect the right and left hemispheres of the CEREBRAL CORTEX.

correlation An association that is found between two VARIABLES.

correlational analysis Testing a HYPOTHESIS using an association that is found between two VARIABLES.

correlation coefficient A statistic (r) that measures the extent to which two VARIABLES are related. It can range from zero CORRELATION to perfect correlation (1.00), where the variables are always associated in the same way, or perfect negative correlation (−1.00), where the variables are always associated but in different ways.

cortex The outer part of an organ, as in the CEREBRAL CORTEX (the outer layer of the BRAIN) and the adrenal cortex.

co-twin control An experimental procedure in which one identical twin (the subject) is given a particular treatment while the other (the control) is not. Used in studies (like IQ or INTELLIGENCE) where the effects of HEREDITY are of particular interest.

counterconditioning   In SYSTEMATIC DESENSITISATION, substituting a relaxation response for a fear response to threatening stimuli.

counterculture   A way of life that is deliberately opposed to and differentiated from the dominant way of life in a society.

counter-stereotype   A positive STEREOTYPE, such as a lawyer in a wheelchair, used to counter the negative effects of stereotyping.

counter-transference   In PSYCHOANALYSIS, the analyst's transference on to his or her patient. Often used more widely to describe the analyst's feelings towards the patient.

criterion group   A group of people of known characteristics, achievement, or behaviour who are used as a standard against which other people are compared in terms of scores on psychological tests. See IQ and INTELLIGENCE TEST.

critical flicker frequency (cff)   The point at which a flickering light no longer appears to flicker but is perceived as a steady light.

critical period   A biologically determined period of time during which an animal is exclusively receptive to certain changes. See IMPRINTING.

critical value   Numerical values found in statistical tables that are used to determine the significance of the observed value produced by a STATISTICAL TEST.

cross-cultural psychology   An approach in which different CULTURES are studied and compared.

cross-cultural variations in attachments   Cross-cultural variations refer to the fact that behaviour, attitudes, norms, and values differ across CULTURES. This is because cultures socially construct different values and norms, etc. Thus the relationships between infants and caregivers vary across cultures because of different childrearing styles and beliefs about which qualities should be nurtured. This is evident in the cross-cultural differences that research has suggested between INDIVIDUALISTIC and COLLECTIVIST cultures.

cross-sectional research   The study of a relatively large and diverse group of people at a single point in time. Compare with LONGITUDINAL RESEARCH and see also COHORT EFFECT.

crowding behaviour   Supposed response of an animal or human to the effects of being crowded, and often subject to very dubious generalisation across species. For example, the aggressive behaviour of rats at a certain level of crowding is thought by many to be instinctive and this "explanation" may then be offered to account for violence in urban slums. There is little or no hard evidence that any human behaviour is instinctive, and as an explanation for the extremely complex (and sometimes apparently contradictory) relationship between urban violence and crowding it is so simplistic as to be silly.

cue-dependent forgetting   Forgetting that occurs because of the absence of a suitable retrieval cue even though the sought-for information is in LONG-TERM MEMORY.

cultural determinism   The viewpoint that the dominant influences in the development of PERSONALITY and the occurrence of particular behaviour patterns are cultural rather than genetically inherited. See also CULTURE.

cultural lag   The continued use of outmoded ways of doing things even after the introduction of more effective means for attaining the particular goals of a society.

cultural relativism   The view that one cannot judge behaviour properly unless it is viewed in the context from which it originates. This is because different CULTURES have different constructions of behaviour and so interpretations of behaviour may differ across cultures. A lack of cultural relativism can lead to ETHNOCENTRISM, where only the perspective of one's own culture is taken.

cultural universality   The notion that a behaviour is unaffected by its cultural context, and that it is the same in every CULTURE.

culture   In the anthropological sense, the rules, morals, and methods of interactions specific to a group of people. To a psychologist, the *unquestioned assumptions* people share about the world, about what is right, wrong, and normal, are perhaps even more important.

culture-bound syndromes   A locality-specific pattern of mental disorder in which a particular syndrome is thought to be specific to a particular CULTURE. There is some debate about whether they really are specific or just local variations on general themes.

culture-free tests   Psychological tests from which the influences or advantages of particular cultural experiences have been eliminated. Such tests, if they could ever be constructed, might therefore be given to anyone anywhere with equal validity.

curve of forgetting   A graphic representation of the rate at which forgetting occurs (Figure 8).

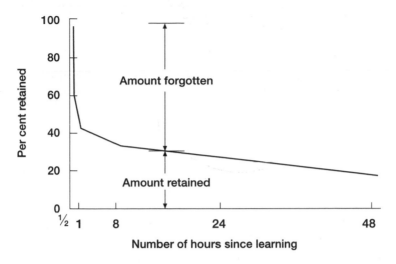

Figure 8   Curve of forgetting

curvilinear relationship   A relationship between two variables depicted graphically by a curve rather than a straight line (Figure 9).

cybernetics   From a Greek term meaning something like "steersman", introduced in 1948 by Norbert Wiener, a computer engineer. It is usually defined briefly as the study of regulatory mechanisms (like thermostats). Out of this field came the analogy of the BRAIN as a computer and the model of psychological processes as systems of messages with their own built-in FEEDBACK.

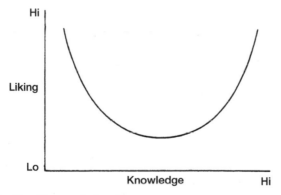

Figure 9   Curvilinear relationship

39

D

dancing mania   A mania that takes the form of wild, uncontrollable dancing. First noticed in the 14th century as an epidemic that raged across Europe in the wake of the Black Death or bubonic plague, apparently as a result of mass religious frenzy combined with some damage to the nervous system from the disease.

dark–light adaptation   The process by which the eyes rapidly adapt to changes in illumination.

Darwin, Charles (1809–1882)   English biologist who presented systematic evidence for the inevitability of evolution and the theory that it is accomplished by a process of NATURAL SELECTION. See also SOCIAL DARWINISM.

Darwinian reflex   A grasping reflex found only in very young animals or human infants.

day care   This refers to care that is provided by people other than the parent or relatives of the infant. It can take different forms, for example, nurseries, childminders, play groups, etc. It is distinct from institutionalised care, which provides permanent substitute care; day care is a temporary alternative to the caregiver.

death instinct   According to FREUD, an UNCONSCIOUS drive towards constriction of the personality, destructiveness, and death. Always contrasted with the LIFE INSTINCT. Taken most seriously by followers of MELANIE KLEIN.

debriefing   Attempts by the experimenter at the end of a study to provide detailed information for the participants about the study and to reduce any distress they might have felt.

decentration   In PIAGET's theory, the ability to focus on more than one aspect of a problem, overcoming the problem of CENTRATION.

deception   This is an ETHICAL GUIDELINE, which states that deception of the participants during the research process should be avoided wherever possible. Deception refers to the withholding of information that might affect the participant's decision to take part in the research. It is an issue because this might lead to psychological harm. Deception is a particularly common issue because the withholding of the RESEARCH HYPOTHESIS is often considered necessary in order to avoid DEMAND CHARACTERISTICS.

decision model   Latané and Darley's model for predicting when an individual will help in an emergency situation, based on a series of decisions to be taken.

decision rule   This refers to the way people make decisions by the conscious or UNCONSCIOUS use of a rule-of-thumb, or HEURISTIC.

declarative knowledge   Factual knowledge. A conscious "knowing that . . ." something is the case. Compare with PROCEDURAL KNOWLEDGE.

decoding   In INFORMATION PROCESSING, the attempt to make sense of a communication by the recipient. Compare with ENCODING.

decortication   Surgical removal of the CEREBRAL CORTEX.

deductive reasoning   The attempt to draw specific conclusions from a given set of assumptions. Compare with INDUCTIVE REASONING.

deep processing   In INFORMATION PROCESSING this refers to the ENCODING of information by an individual in a way that is meaningful to him or her.

defence mechanisms   Strategies used by the EGO to defend itself against ANXIETY.

defensive attribution   A concept important in both CLINICAL and SOCIAL PSYCHOLOGY which refers to the tendency to blame the victim of a frightening misfortune as a way of avoiding the anxiety-provoking thought that one could be in the victim's place. For example "rape victims ask for it". See also JUST-WORLD HYPOTHESIS.

deferred imitation   In PIAGET's theory, the ability to imitate behaviour that was observed at an earlier time.

definition of the situation   This refers to the way someone perceives and interprets the nature of the SOCIAL INTERACTION in which he or she participates; associated with the dictum of the American sociologist W. I. Thomas that "if human beings define situations as real, they are real in their consequences".

dehumanisation   The process of treating other people as something other than human. Often done out of fear and with the purpose of reducing guilt about aggressive behaviour. See DIABOLISM.

deindividuation   Losing a sense of personal identity that may occur, e.g., when in a crowd or wearing a mask. See COLLECTIVE MIND and CONTAGION THEORY OF CROWDS.

déjà vu   Literally, "already seen" in French. The illusion of recognising something although it is a new experience. Perhaps due to a disturbance of the brain's MEMORY functions.

delayed gratification Sociological term for the act of forgoing present satisfaction for the sake of greater satisfaction some time in the future. For example, saving money rather than spending it. Supposed to be more typical of the middle classes than any other group in our society.

delayed reciprocal altruism One individual performs a favour for another on the assumption that the favour will be returned later on (also known as RECIPROCITY).

delinquency Usually used in connection with teenagers—and often called "juvenile delinquency"—to describe breaches of the law like theft and vandalism. Many factors have been proposed to explain it over the years, such as depressing environment, unhappy home life, innate sinfulness, and the SELF-FULFILLING PROPHECY engendered by LABELLING.

delirium An ALTERED STATE OF CONSCIOUSNESS characterised by DELUSIONS, HALLUCINATIONS, and ILLUSIONS.

delirium tremens A delirium suffered by chronic alcoholics after withdrawal of alcohol. A classic WITHDRAWAL SYMPTOM.

delta waves Large, slow BRAIN WAVES occurring about three a second. Found only in deep sleep.

delusion A false belief that is impervious to evidence or reason. Often a symptom of PSYCHOSIS.

delusions of grandeur The delusion that one is a celebrated or exalted person.

delusions of persecution An individual's delusion that their problems are caused by other people conspiring against them.

demand characteristics Features of an experimental situation that help participants to work out what is expected of them, and "invite" them to behave in certain predictable ways. See also EXPERIMENTER BIAS.

dementia A disabling disorder of both COGNITION and AFFECT that impairs the higher mental processes of learning, thinking, decision-making, and especially MEMORY, and is accompanied by changes in PERSONALITY and ways of relating to other people.

denial The DEFENCE MECHANISM whereby someone refuses to accept either the occurrence of a painful experience or the existence of an anxiety-provoking impulse.

dependence Used in at least three senses (and sometimes written "dependency"). (1) In science generally, if one thing is thought to be caused by another it is said to be dependent on it. (2) In CLINICAL

PSYCHOLOGY a person is said to be dependent on someone or something to the extent that they need that person or thing in order to go about their regular activities. (3) In SOCIAL PSYCHOLOGY it is sometimes used to refer to the way in which people in a group rely on each other for a definition of reality.

dependent variable In EXPERIMENTAL PSYCHOLOGY, the variable whose state is one of dependence on the INDEPENDENT VARIABLE. The independent variable, manipulated by the experimenter, constitutes the stimulus and the dependent variable the response. Any changes measured in the response are attributed to the effects of the stimulus.

depenetration Deliberately reducing the amount of self-disclosure to someone else.

depression One of the most common forms of emotional disturbance, which can vary in intensity from an everyday attack of "the blues" to a psychotic condition of paralysing hopelessness. It is characterised by ANXIETY, dejection and a general lowering of activity. There is a difference of opinion as to whether (or to what extent) the causes of depression are to be found in UNCONSCIOUS conflict or in biochemical malfunctioning of the BRAIN. See also ANACLITIC DEPRESSION.

deprivation To lose something, such as the care of an ATTACHMENT figure for a period of time.

deprivation dwarfism Physical underdevelopment found in children reared in isolation or in institutions. Thought to be an effect of the STRESS associated with emotional DEPRIVATION.

depth interview A situation in which the interviewer tries to get beyond the conscious responses of the interviewee to probe UNCONSCIOUS feelings.

depth of processing American term for LEVELS OF PROCESSING.

depth perception The awareness of how far distant objects are from the eye and the ability to perceive the world as three dimensional, i.e., as having depth as well as height and width.

depth psychology The study of the part the UNCONSCIOUS plays in human behaviour. See also DYNAMIC PSYCHOLOGY.

derived etic Using a series of emic studies to build up a picture of a particular CULTURE. See EMIC CONSTRUCTS.

descriptive statistics Statistics that summarise or describe a set of measurements, e.g., MEASURES OF CENTRAL TENDENCY. Compare with INFERENTIAL STATISTICS.

43

desensitisation The process of becoming less sensitive to stimuli the more they are encountered.

determinism The view that all behaviour is caused by factors other than one's own will.

developmental psychology The branch of psychology that deals with the interactions of physical, psychological, and social changes that occur as an individual increases in age. For a long time this meant largely childhood development and perhaps adolescence but increasing attention is now being paid to MIDDLESCENCE and SENESCENCE.

developmental tasks Skills and achievements that are considered necessary for children to attain at certain ages to ensure their psychological well-being, e.g., walking, talking, reading.

deviance amplification effect The creation of unrealistic NORMS, for example that the world is more dangerous than it really is.

deviant Someone whose behaviour violates prevailing NORMS of morality in his or her society.

deviation A departure from the NORM. In STATISTICS, the difference of a given score from the MEAN.

deviation from ideal mental health Deviation from optimal psychological well-being (a state of contentment that we all strive to achieve). Deviation is characterised by a lack of positive self-attitudes, personal growth, autonomy, accurate view of reality, environmental mastery, and resistance to STRESS; all of which prevent individuals from accessing their potential, which is known as SELF-ACTUALISATION.

deviation from social norms Behaviour that does not follow socially accepted patterns; violation of them is considered ABNORMAL. These unwritten social rules are culturally relative and era-dependent. For example, HOMOSEXUALITY was once illegal and considered to be a mental disorder because it deviated from the social norm. Now there are campaigns for gay marriages to be recognised and afforded the same benefits as heterosexual marriages, and this shows the extent to which this definition of abnormality is subject to change.

diabolism Attributing to a person or group the attributes of the Devil. A process of DEHUMANISATION frequently encountered in wartime where there is a powerful need to assuage ANXIETY and GUILT by making the enemy all bad and one's own side all good.

Diagnostic and Statistical Manual (DSM)   A multiaxial system used for classifying and diagnosing over 200 mental disorders, published by the American Psychiatric Association. DSM-IV is the most recent version.

diagnostic test   An instrument used by psychologists for probing the nature of a mental or emotional difficulty. See PROJECTIVE TECHNIQUES.

diathesis–stress model   The notion that psychological disorders occur when there is a genetically determined vulnerability (diathesis) and relevant stressful conditions.

dichotic listening task   An attention task in which one auditory message is presented to one ear and a different message is presented to the other ear.

difference limen   See JUST NOTICEABLE DIFFERENCE.

differential threshold   See JUST NOTICEABLE DIFFERENCE.

differentiation   In CONDITIONING, a procedure whereby an animal is trained to distinguish between two similar stimuli or two similar responses.

diffusion of responsibility   If there are many observers of an incident, each person feels they bear only a small portion of the blame for not helping. See BYSTANDER APATHY.

digit-span test   A way of testing a person's MEMORY span by asking him or her to recall a series of random numbers or digits after a single hearing. Most people can recall seven digits, on average.

diminishing returns   An idea borrowed from economics to describe an improvement that gets progressively smaller with each succeeding increment. In PSYCHOLOGY it is used in the study of LEARNING and MEMORY where, after a large gain at the beginning, extra practice begins to provide less and less gain.

dimorphism   The existence of two forms, such as male and female forms of the same species.

dipsomania   A MANIA that takes the form of a periodic craving for alcohol. Unlike chronic alcoholism the patient is not dependent on a daily intake of alcohol and his or her bouts of drinking are thought to be symptomatic of a deep-lying emotional disorder.

direct fitness   Fitness in terms of GENE survival gained through production of offspring.

directional (one-tailed) hypothesis   A prediction that there will be a difference or correlation between the two VARIABLES *and* a statement of the direction of this difference.

45

discounting principle A HEURISTIC for making ATTRIBUTIONS in which an observer attaches less importance to one potential cause of behaviour when other more obvious potential causes are also present.

discourse analysis Qualitative analysis of spoken and written communications produced in fairly natural conditions; usually based on tape recordings.

discrimination (1) In LEARNING THEORY, the CONDITIONED RESPONSE to one CONDITIONED STIMULUS is strengthened at the same time as that to a second conditioned stimulus is weakened. (2) In SOCIAL PSYCHOLOGY, the behaviour (usually negative) that results from prejudiced attitudes and which is directed at members of some particular group.

disinhibition Loss of INHIBITIONS.

disintegration Literally, the loss of integration or organisation of something whose parts usually fit together harmoniously. In PSYCH-OLOGY it is used most often about PERSONALITY whose thinking, feeling and acting components can disintegrate under the STRESS of severe psychological disturbance. See also PSYCHOSIS.

disorganised attachment (type D) The infant shows no set pattern of behaviour at separation or reunion (thus "disorganised"). This kind of behaviour is associated with abused children or those whose mothers are chronically depressed.

displacement The pushing out of information from SHORT-TERM MEMORY by new information before it has been processed for long enough to pass on to LONG-TERM MEMORY.

display In ETHOLOGY, the concept that a male animal will show itself off to the best advantage either to fight or to woo when it is approached by the appropriate stimulus of a male or female of the same species. The concept is often applied to human adolescent behaviour.

display rules Sometimes used in SOCIOLOGY to indicate behaviour designed to mask real feelings by presenting what appears to be a different feeling.

dispositional attributions/explanations Deciding that other people's actions are caused by their internal characteristics or dispositions.

dissociation (1) For the individual, a situation in which a set of integrated psychological processes split off from the rest of an individual's PERSONALITY and appear to take on an independent existence of their own. (2) For the group, minority ideas absorbed into the majority viewpoint without anyone remembering where they came from.

dissociative disorders A group of mental illnesses where patients experience dissociation between areas of conscious behaviour, as in MULTIPLE PERSONALITY DISORDER (DISSOCIATIVE IDENTITY DISORDER) and dissociative AMNESIA.

dissociative identity disorder A condition characterised by the existence of more than two identities that recurrently take control of an individual's behaviour and by the occurrence of episodes of lost recall, none of which can be explained by physical causes.

distributed cognition The idea that the achievement of many social goals is only possible through the collaboration of different people with shared values who pool their knowledge and ideas. Compare with PARALLEL DISTRIBUTED PROCESSING.

distributed control The concept that major functions are controlled by many different areas of the BRAIN with diffuse interconnections, in contrast to the concept of LOCALISATION.

distributed practice A technique of LEARNING in which the lessons or periods of practice are spread out as widely as the available time permits. A much more effective method of learning than MASSED PRACTICE with which it is usually contrasted.

distribution Statistical term for the arrangement of data in categories and their display in the form of a group or table, like a NORMAL DISTRIBUTION. (See Figure 13.)

distributive justice A situation in which everyone receives a just reward. Even though this situation rarely occurs in real life, it has been suggested that people need to operate on the basis of a JUST-WORLD HYPOTHESIS.

divergent thinking Creative and original thinking that deviates from the obvious and the conventional to produce several possible solutions to a particular problem. Contrasted with CONVERGENT THINKING. See also LATERAL THINKING.

dizygotic twins Fraternal twins derived from two fertilised ova and therefore sharing 50% of their GENES with each other. Contrast with MONOZYGOTIC TWINS.

dominance Used of a person with a strong need to control or be more important than other people. See also DOMINANT GENE and CEREBRAL DOMINANCE.

dominant gene The appearance in an offspring of a certain

47

physical characteristic as a result of one factor dominating the other with which it is paired in a parental GENE. See RECESSIVE GENE.

Doppler effect   The increase or decrease in light waves or sound waves as the source of the light or sound approaches or recedes from an observer. For example, a car horn as it rushes past is perceived as changing its pitch.

double-bind theory   Based on the idea that receiving contradictory messages from an authority figure can feel like an impossible situation for the recipient. Used as an explanation for SCHIZO-PHRENIA that suggests the disorder is a learned response to mutually exclusive demands, which cannot be met or avoided, being made on a child. See also EXPERIMENTAL NEUROSIS.

double-blind technique   An experimental method in which neither the subject nor the experimenter is aware of the point at which the experimental manipulation is introduced. Used especially of experiments with drugs where neither subject nor experimenter knows which drug is being administered when and to whom. The technique is an attempt to overcome the conscious and unconscious effects of EXPERIMENTER BIAS.

Down's syndrome   A form of CONGENITAL MENTAL RETARDATION that is due to a genetic abnormality. Apparently Down's syndrome occurs most frequently in children of older mothers.

Draw-a-Person Test   A PROJECTIVE TECHNIQUE in which young children are asked to draw a person as a gross test of intellectual ability or MENTAL RETARDATION. It is also used in research on the SELF-CONCEPT.

dream   Imagery that occurs during sleep, usually with a certain coherence but sometimes with bizarre, unusual or confusing aspects as well.

dream interpretation   A basic technique of PSYCHOANALYSIS where the FREE ASSOCIATION of the patient to the various elements of his or her dreams is employed in an attempt to understand their hidden meaning. FREUD regarded dreams as "the royal road to the unconscious", and as no activity of the UNCONSCIOUS is random or meaningless the symbolism to be found in a dream represented an important clue to the patient's underlying MOTIVATION. See also LATENT CONTENT and MANIFEST CONTENT.

dream sleep   In the 1950s it was discovered that RAPID EYE MOVEMENTS (REMs) were associated with dreaming, thus providing a possibility for studying the biological functions of DREAMS experimentally. This experimental work appears to support FREUD's contention that dreams are an essential part of psychological functioning. When people are awakened during REM SLEEP and thus deprived of their dreams, they seem to experience signs of psychological disturbance. Whereas Freud asserted that the dream functions to keep the dreamer asleep by transforming his or her unacceptable wishes into a more comfortable form, some experimenters would argue that the reverse is more nearly true, that the function of sleep is actually to allow one to dream. Some people can function well on relatively little sleep but all human beings (and even higher animals) appear to have a biological need to dream when they are asleep.

dream wish   In PSYCHOANALYSIS, the form in which a repressed wish appears in a dream. See WISH-FULFILMENT.

dream work   In PSYCHOANALYSIS, the process by which the desires of the ID are converted in the UNCONSCIOUS into acceptable material for dreams.

drive reduction   The weakening of a DRIVE in an animal or human, usually as a result of the appropriate needs being satisfied.

drives   The motivational forces that make individuals active and lead them to pursue certain goals. See INSTINCT and MOTIVATION.

DTs   See DELIRIUM TREMENS.

dual personality   The simplest form of MULTIPLE PERSONALITY, like Jekyll and Hyde. A form of DISSOCIATIVE IDENTITY DISORDER.

duration   This refers to how long a MEMORY lasts. The existence of two distinct memory stores is supported by duration because this differs between STM and LTM. STM has a very limited duration of 18–30 seconds, whereas LTM potentially lasts forever and so a memory may endure permanently.

DV (dependent variable)   An aspect of the participant's behaviour that is measured in the study.

dyad   A two-person group.

dynamic psychology   Those aspects of psychology that are concerned with MOTIVATION and with understanding the underlying causes of behaviour in all its ramifications. PSYCHOANALYSIS and psychoanalytically influenced areas of psychology are the prime, but not the only, examples of dynamic psychology: GESTALT PSYCHOLOGY would also qualify, for instance.

dyslexia   An impairment of word perception involving a loss of ability to read or understand words. Contrast with ALEXIA.

E

eating disorder A dysfunctional relationship with food. The dysfunction may be gross under-eating (ANOREXIA), binge–purging (BULIMIA), over-eating (obesity), or even healthy eating (orthorexia). These disorders may be characterised by faulty COGNITION and emotional responses to food, maladaptive CONDITIONING, dysfunctional family relationships, early childhood conflicts, or a biological and genetic basis, but the nature and expression of eating disorders show great individual variation.

echoic response A term used by SKINNER to describe imitation of another's verbalisations; an aspect of the process of language acquisition.

echoic store A sensory MEMORY that lasts for a second or two following an auditory stimulus. The auditory equivalent of an ICONIC STORE.

echolalia The meaningless and involuntary repetition of words or phrases that someone else has just said. Usually a sign of PSYCHOSIS or serious BRAIN DAMAGE.

echolocation A technique for locating objects in the environment by emitting sound waves and then perceiving them as they reflect back off the objects. This technique, which is the basis of sonar systems for detecting objects in the water, has been learned from the behaviour of whales and bats. Blind people use it, often without realising it, when they tap their sticks on walls or floors. The echoes they hear allow them to locate objects around them.

eclectic approach Any approach in PSYCHOLOGY that draws on many different perspectives.

ecological validity The validity of the RESEARCH outside the research situation itself; the extent to which the findings are generalisable to other situations, especially "everyday" situations. The question is whether you would get the same findings in a different setting or whether they are limited to the original research context. If the latter is true then there is a lack of EXTERNAL VALIDITY.

ECT See ELECTRO-CONVULSIVE THERAPY

EEG See ELECTROENCEPHALOGRAM.

effective stimulus A stimulus that produces a response when applied to an appropriate sense receptor. For example, shining a light in front of a subject's eye would probably be an effective stimulus; shining it at the subject's back probably would not.

efferent The process of transmitting nervous impulses *from* the BRAIN through the nervous system to the glands and muscles. Contrasted with AFFERENT.

efficacy A term sometimes used in SOCIAL PSYCHOLOGY to indicate how effective a person feels in influencing matters of importance to him or her.

ego The conscious, rational mind; one of the three main parts of the mind in FREUD's theory. See ID and SUPEREGO.

ego analysis A form of therapy developed from PSYCHOANALYSIS that focuses on strengthening the EGO.

egocentric speech A term used by Vygotsky to indicate that young children's speech is often self-centred and like inner speech.

egocentrism The sense of being the centre of everything and that one's view is the only view.

ego defence See DEFENCE MECHANISM.

ego ideal In PSYCHOANALYSIS, a part of the SUPEREGO that represents an identification with parents or parent figures who are admired and loved.

ego psychology An emphasis found in post-Freudian psychoanalytic theory which gives more importance to the functions of the EGO and its relations to external reality than FREUD had done.

ego strength The ability of an individual to maintain the EGO in its function of avoiding emotional disturbance and maladjustment.

eidetic imagery Commonly known as photographic MEMORY. Exceptionally vivid (usually visual) imagery of objects or events that have previously been experienced. The images are as clear as if the subjects were perceiving them still. The ability to experience eidetic imagery is common, if not universal, in young children but in most people it disappears with age.

elaborated code In Bernstein's theory, complex and abstract language. Contrast with RESTRICTED CODE.

elaborative rehearsal A strategy for remembering information that fosters the association of new LEARNING with existing learning, or with other new information, to make it more meaningful. Contrast with ROTE LEARNING.

Electra complex The suggestion, in PSYCHOANALYSIS, that girls experience something similar to the OEDIPUS COMPLEX, where a young girl desires her father and sees her mother as a rival.

electro-convulsive therapy (ECT)   A technique, used mainly in treating severe DEPRESSION, of producing behavioural changes by passing an electrical current briefly through a patient's BRAIN. The technique causes muscular convulsions and renders the patient unconscious. It is claimed that the patient's depression can often be eased in this way but nobody knows why—nor whether there are any permanent long-term side-effects. Nowadays the patient is usually given a sedative and a muscle-relaxing drug before ECT to reduce the dangers of physical damage occurring. Commonly known as "shock treatment" and considered barbaric by many psychologists.

electrodes   A piece of metal or other material that conducts electricity from one place to another.

electroencephalogram (EEG)   Electrical BRAIN potentials recorded via ELECTRODES placed on the scalp.

elementary mental functions   INNATE capacities, such as attention and sensation. Such functions are possessed by all animals and these will develop to a limited extent through experience.

embedded figure   A figure concealed within a more complex figure. Once detected it is difficult to ignore. (Figure 10.)

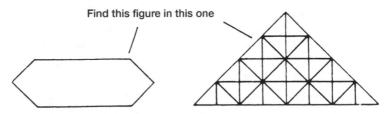

Figure 10   Embedded figure

emic constructs   Those that vary from one CULTURE to another.

emotion   In the way psychologists use this term there is widespread agreement that it represents a complex state of diffuse physical changes, marked by strong feelings and accompanied by a behavioural impulse towards achieving a specific goal. The identification and labelling of particular emotions involves a large element of social learning and varies widely across time and place.

empathic joy hypothesis   The notion that when people help a needy person they share that person's joy at being helped.

empathy   The ability to understand someone else's point of view, and to share their emotions.

empathy–altruism hypothesis Batson's notion that ALTRUISM is largely motivated by EMPATHY.

empirical A finding based on experience or observation; the basis for experimental science.

empiricism The view that all behaviour is the consequence of experience. The extreme "nurture" side of the NATURE–NURTURE DEBATE.

encephalitis An inflammation of the BRAIN, usually through an infectious disease. Sometimes results in personality changes including what appears to be a lowering of INTELLIGENCE.

encoding The transfer of information into code, which creates a MEMORY trace that can be registered in the memory store. STM and LTM are dependent on different codes, as in STM encoding is primarily acoustic (based on the sound of the word) and in LTM encoding is primarily semantic (based on the meaning of the word).

encounter group A group that uses SENSITIVITY TRAINING.

endocrine system A system of a number of ductless glands located throughout the body that produce the body's chemical messengers, called HORMONES.

endogamy The practice of restricting marriage partners to a person from one's own social or kinship group. Contrasted with EXOGAMY.

endogenous Internally caused, as distinct from external causes. Contrasted with EXOGENOUS.

endogenous depression DEPRESSION resulting from internal, biological causes, as distinct from REACTIVE DEPRESSION.

endorphins A group of chemical agents produced naturally by the BRAIN or the pituitary gland which have opiate-like effects in reducing pain and increasing pleasure.

engineering psychology An American term for ERGONOMICS.

engram A hypothetical biochemical memory trace or physical representation of MEMORY. Many psychologists have long assumed that the process of LEARNING and remembering results in some physical changes in BRAIN tissue, although no one has actually observed these changes.

enmeshment A situation in which all of the members of a family lack a clear sense of their own personal IDENTITY.

entraining Synchronising two or more things.

entrapment In SOCIAL PSYCHOLOGY the process of escalating commitment to a course of action in order to justify an initial investment in it. People may then feel trapped but find it increasingly difficult to break free. Derived from COGNITIVE DISSONANCE theory.

enuresis Involuntary release of urine, such as bed-wetting in children, usually from emotional disturbance rather than organic causes.

environment of evolutionary adaptation (EEA) The period in human evolution during which our GENES were shaped and naturally selected to solve survival problems that were operating at that time (between 35,000 and 3 million years ago).

environmental determinism The view that all behaviour can be explained solely in terms of the effects of external (environmental) factors.

environmental-stress theory A sociological interpretation of what psychologists would refer to as NEUROSIS, which is attributed to the distorting effect of a particular environment on behaviour tendencies common to everyone.

epigenesis A biological theory about the development of the embryo which stresses the influence of the environment. The interaction of embryo and environment produces new properties that were not present in the fertilised egg, or ZYGOTE. In certain psychological theories, especially those of ERIK ERIKSON, epigenesis refers to a sequence of development stages that must be followed to attain psychological maturity.

epilepsy Disturbances in the electrical activity of the BRAIN caused by neurological disorder. In the severe form, or grand mal, the patient may suffer violent convulsions and prolonged loss of consciousness. In the mild form, or petit mal, the seizure may produce only a momentary dizziness or loss of consciousness. Anticonvulsant drugs can often control the grand mal seizures but the causes of epilepsy, a disease known for thousands of years as the "falling sickness", are still not fully understood.

epiphenomenon In the philosophy of MIND, an event that accompanies another event without having any causal relationship to it.

episodic memory A memory of personal significance that includes the circumstances in which a particular episode (event) occurred. Compare with SEMANTIC MEMORY.

epistemology The branch of philosophy that deals with the search for true knowledge; the origins, nature, limits, and verifiability of what is known.

equal-status contact   Considered essential by social scientists in breaking down social PREJUDICES. Mere contact between different groups, as in the CONTACT HYPOTHESIS, apparently just intensifies pre-existing prejudices.

equilibration   Using the processes of ACCOMMODATION and of ASSIMILATION to produce a state of equilibrium or balance.

equipotentiality   The view that essentially any response can be conditioned to any stimulus.

ergonomics   The study of the interaction between people and their work environment, particularly their relationship to machines and equipment. As well as PSYCHOLOGY it draws on anatomy and physiology.

Erikson, Erik (1902–1979)   A PSYCHOANALYST usually classified as neo-Freudian because of his emphasis on EGO psychology. Erikson had an overriding interest in problems of identity. He proposed the principle of EPIGENESIS, that there is a sequence of eight stages of development, all of them with crucial psychological tasks to be achieved and through each of which an individual must successfully pass in order to attain maturity. The most crucial of these periods is that of ADOLESCENCE, when the individual is in the process of forming an IDENTITY through the activity of the EGO or conscious SELF.

   Erikson's concern with IDENTITY CRISES led him to examine those of various historical figures, and his work on Martin Luther generated a lot of interest in the field of PSYCHOHISTORY. In general Erikson has influenced numerous workers in the field of human development to discount the exclusive Freudian focus on childhood and pay more serious attention to adolescence—and, to a lesser extent, the entire LIFE CYCLE.

erogenous zones   Areas of the body whose stimulation is particularly prone to result in sexual arousal. The all-time favourites would appear to be genitals, mouth, and breasts, but this may be partly because they've had a better press (as it were) than other parts.

Eros   The Greek god of love, used by FREUD to symbolise the LIBIDO or self-preserving drive for life. Contrasted with THANATOS.

ESP   See EXTRASENSORY PERCEPTION.

estrogen   See OESTROGEN

ethical guidelines   A written code of conduct designed to aid psychologists when designing and running their research. The guidelines set out standards of what is and is not acceptable. The code focuses on the need to treat participants with respect and to not cause them harm or distress. For example, the BPS code of conduct advises of "the need to preserve an overriding high regard for the well-being and dignity of research participants" (BPS 1993).

ethical issues   Ethical issues arise in the implementing of research when there is conflict between how the research should be carried out (e.g., with no DECEPTION to the participants) and the methodological consequences of observing this (e.g., reduced VALIDITY of the findings). Another issue is that of participants versus society. Is it justifiable to infringe upon the rights of participants if the research will be of benefit to society? Such issues are an inevitable consequence of researching people and resolving the issues can be difficult.

ethnic groups   Cultural groups (e.g., those defined by race or religion) living within a larger society.

ethnic identity   (1) The ethnic group one identifies with or is identified by. (2) Where one's ethnic group forms an important part of personal IDENTITY.

ethnocentrism   The belief that one's own ethnic or cultural group is more important than other ethnic or cultural groups.

ethnographics   Making comparisons between CULTURES with a view to learning more about a target culture, in a similar way to how COMPARATIVE PSYCHOLOGY can enlighten us about human behaviour.

ethological approach   The study of animal behaviour in natural environments; this approach emphasises the importance of inherited capacities and responses.

ethology   The biological study of animal behaviour, which seeks to determine the functional value of behaviours and tends to rely on naturalistic observation.

etic constructs   Universal factors that hold across CULTURES.

etiology   See AETIOLOGY.

eugenics   A branch of applied genetics that attempts to improve the inherited qualities of a species by selective breeding. When the species concerned is *homo sapiens* the goals, values, criteria, and methods of eugenics immediately become ethical questions— which have been debated since Plato first proposed them in the fourth century BC.

Eurocentric   Believing that European CULTURE and behaviour is superior to, or more natural than, other cultures.

euthanasia   The practice of "mercy killing", terminating a pain-filled life with a painless death.

evoked potentials   The average pattern in the EEG produced when a stimulus is presented several times.

evolution   A gradual process of genetic development and change in animal life over many generations. Those members of a species best adapted to their environment in any generation (i.e., the "fittest") have the best chance of surviving and reproducing successfully. See DARWIN, NATURAL SELECTION, and SURVIVAL VALUE.

evolutionarily stable strategy   A behaviour or strategy that persists because it cannot be bettered.

evolutionary   Following the theory of evolution, that certain behaviours are adaptive otherwise they would not have survived the process of NATURAL SELECTION.

evolutionary psychiatry   An application of the evolutionary approach to treating mental disorders through understanding the function of the behaviours involved in the disorder.

evolutionary psychology   An approach that explains behaviour in terms of its function and adaptiveness (i.e., the extent to which a behaviour enhances survival and reproduction of the individual's GENES).

exchange theory   A way of explaining the relationship between two people in a DYAD. It is mainly concerned with examining the relative rewards and costs of the relationship for each individual. The theory was introduced to SOCIAL PSYCHOLOGY by John Thibaut and Harold Kelley.

exchange theory of friendship   A sociological concept of friendship using the economic terminology of the market place where people estimate their "worth" and look for people of equal or greater worth to exchange friendship with.

exhibitionism   A compulsion to expose oneself in public, either literally or metaphorically.

existential psychiatry   A movement that rejects the MEDICAL MODEL for the treatment of mental illness in favour of trying to analyse the conscious self of the disturbed individual. Such a person is not treated as a patient to be cured but rather as an individual to be understood and to be helped in achieving self-understanding. See also LAING.

existential psychology   A movement or school that views the task of psychology as an understanding of CONSCIOUSNESS and the

contents of the MIND. The basic method of this school is INTROSPEC-
TION, the concentration on immediate awareness. This is sup-
posedly a growing emphasis in psychology although it goes back to
WILHELM WUNDT in the 19th century.

exogamy   The practice of restricting marriage partners to a person
from outside one's own social or kinship group. Contrasted with
ENDOGAMY.

exogenous   Based on factors external to the organism. Contrasted
with ENDOGENOUS.

expected utility   The anticipated value of each option's outcome.

experiment   A procedure undertaken to make a discovery about
causal relationships. The experimenter manipulates one VARIABLE
(the INDEPENDENT VARIABLE) to see its effect on another variable (the
DEPENDENT VARIABLE).

experimental design   Technically, the investigation of the way in
which the INDEPENDENT VARIABLE in an experiment affects the
DEPENDENT VARIABLE, but used generally for the whole procedure
of an experiment, from the selection of subjects to the statistical
analysis of the results.

experimental extinction   In CONDITIONING, the loss of a learned
response. In CLASSICAL CONDITIONING this happens when the CON-
DITIONED STIMULUS is no longer accompanied by the UNCONDITIONED
STIMULUS. In OPERANT CONDITIONING it happens when the response is
no longer reinforced.

experimental group   Subjects in an experiment who are exposed
to the EXPERIMENTAL VARIABLE and whose behaviour is expected to
be influenced by it. Contrasted with the CONTROL GROUP which is
not exposed to the experimental variable.

experimental hypothesis   The HYPOTHESIS written prior to conducting an EXPERIMENT which usually specifies the DEPENDENT and
INDEPENDENT VARIABLES.

experimental neurosis   Disturbed behaviour of animals in an
experiment when they are faced with an impossible problem. This
phenomenon was discovered by PAVLOV when he rewarded a dog
with food for responding (by salivating) to a circle and then with-
held the reward when the stimulus was an ellipse. Pavlov gradually
made the two stimuli more and more alike. When the point was
reached at which the dog could no longer discriminate the circle
from the ellipse the animal lashed out in a frenzy of wild and
random behaviour. Whether this behaviour can be equated with
human NEUROSIS is a matter of long-standing dispute among
psychologists.

experimental psychology   The use of experimental methods to study psychological phenomena.

experimental realism   A term sometimes used in SOCIAL PSYCH-OLOGY to denote the attempt to capture the essential elements of a real-life situation in an experimental form rather than trying to reconstruct the real-life situation (or MUNDANE REALISM) exactly. See, for example, PRISONER'S DILEMMA.

experimental validity   The extent to which research has INTERNAL and EXTERNAL VALIDITY. Internal validity refers to the extent to which the experiment measured what it set out to, i.e., is the observed effect in the DV a result of the manipulation of the IV? External validity refers to the generalisability of the findings to other settings (ecological), or POPULATIONS and periods in time (temporal). Any threats to internal or external validity reduce the meaningfulness of the findings.

experimental variable   Technically the name given to the INDEPENDENT VARIABLE when it can be manipulated by an experimenter. In practice the terms are often used interchangeably.

experimenter bias   The effects on an EXPERIMENT of the conscious or unconscious attempts by the experimenter to influence the outcome in the direction he or she has predicted. An important and pervasive problem, as the outcome of virtually every published experiment is in the predicted direction. The ramifications of this phenomenon are much wider than the experimental situation. See also DEMAND CHARACTERISTICS, DOUBLE-BLIND TECHNIQUE, INTERVIEWER BIAS, ROSENTHAL EFFECT, and SELF-FULFILLING PROPHECY.

experts   People with greater knowledge of a subject than oneself. This can include peers.

expiatory punishment   The view that the amount of punishment should match the badness of behaviour, but without the idea that the form of punishment should fit the crime.

explicit memory   The conscious and explicit recollection of something This form of memory is usually what is lost in AMNESIA, unlike IMPLICIT MEMORY.

expressed emotion   A way of describing the behaviour of certain families. These behaviours include too much criticism, hostility, and emotional over-protectiveness.

extended family   Defined differently for different societies but always includes more distant relations (both genetically and geographically) than the NUCLEAR FAMILY with which it is contrasted.

externalisation   Used in various ways that sometimes shade into each other, e.g., regarding one's thoughts and feelings as being caused by some external agency; projecting one's thoughts and feelings on to the external world; seeing one's own mental processes as being outside one's own mind (as a HALLUCINATION); the process that occurs throughout childhood of separating off one's sense of self from the external world; EGO formation in Freudian terms.

external validity   The validity of an EXPERIMENT outside the research situation itself; the extent to which the findings of a research study are applicable to other situations, especially "everyday" situations. Compare with INTERNAL VALIDITY.

extrapunitive   Characteristically reacting to frustration by behaving aggressively towards the people or objects seen as causing the frustration. Contrast with INTROPUNITIVE.

extrasensory perception (ESP)   The ability to receive information about the world from sources other than the known senses. Whether or not such abilities exist is still a matter of great debate among psychologists. See CLAIRVOYANCE, PRECOGNITION, PSYCHOKINESIS, and TELEPATHY, all of which are regarded as branches of ESP by people interested in PARAPSYCHOLOGY.

extraversion   According to JUNG, a basic PERSONALITY dimension of openness and outward-looking sociability that is usually contrasted with INTROVERSION.

extrinsic   A feature that lies outside the organism, i.e., is external.

extrinsic motivation   Doing something for reasons of reward or punishment external to the activity itself, like gaining or losing money. Always contrasted with INTRINSIC MOTIVATION. See also FUNCTIONAL AUTONOMY.

eye contact   People looking each other in the eye. A form of behaviour studied by social scientists as a way of understanding interpersonal distance and relationships in different social situations, both in our own CULTURE, and comparatively, across cultures.

eyewitness testimony   Evidence supplied by people who witness a specific event or crime, relying only on their MEMORY. Statements often include descriptions of the criminal (facial appearance and other identifiable characteristics) and subsequent identification, and details of the crime scene (e.g., the sequence of events, time of day, and if others witnessed the event, etc.). There is good evidence that eyewitness testimony can be incorrect, because eyewitness memories of events tend to be fragile and easily distorted (e.g., by leading questions).

Eysenck, H. J. (1916–1997) A leading British exponent of behaviourist psychology noted for his contributions to the theory of PERSONALITY and the construction of personality tests. He has been a controversial figure in the debate about RACE and IQ.

F

F (Fascism) Scale A test of tendencies towards fascism. See AUTHORITARIAN PERSONALITY.

fabulation Telling fantastic stories as though they were true— although not involuntarily as in the case of people suffering disturbances of MEMORY (CONFABULATION).

face recognition Concerned with the processes involved in the way we recognise faces. An increasingly important area of research in COGNITION and PERCEPTION.

face-to-face group In SOCIAL PSYCHOLOGY, a term for a small group of people in close enough physical proximity for each person in the group to interact directly with each of the others. Such a group is usually no more than six to eight people.

face validity The extent to which a psychological test or other procedure appears relevant to the VARIABLE it is dealing with.

facework In SOCIAL PSYCHOLOGY, sometimes used to describe social rituals that save "face" or enhance a public image at the expense of honest emotion.

facilitation Making things easier; it is used in reference either to the performance of a given behaviour or the transmission of a nerve impulse. See SOCIAL FACILITATION.

factor analysis A statistical technique for analysing complex CORRELATIONS of scores and tracing the factors underlying these correlations.

failure to function adequately A model of ABNORMALITY based on an inability to cope with day-to-day life caused by psychological distress or discomfort.

faith healing The attempt to heal sickness through a non-rational belief without medical means being used. This belief is usually religious, such as the belief in the healing power of the Virgin Mary by the people who make a pilgrimage to Lourdes. But people can also have faith in their doctor, even when he or she has no medicine to help them, or in themselves and their own powers of recovery. There are perhaps some grounds for believing that faith healing can affect PSYCHOSOMATIC illness; that it can affect organic illness is more dubious.

false memory syndrome   A condition where an adult "recovers" apparently repressed memories. In fact the memories are of events that did not happen, hence "false memory". See RECOVERED MEMORY.

falsifiability   The notion that scientific theories can potentially be disproved by evidence; it is the hallmark of science, according to Popper.

family therapy   Where the family rather than the individual is in PSYCHOTHERAPY, on the assumption that an observed individual NEUROSIS is the product of disturbed relationships between family members.

fantasy   A deliberate act of the imagination in which it is given free rein, usually to experience enjoyable images related to one's wish fulfilment. Drug-induced fantasy may be very unpleasant, however.

father figure   Someone who is seen as standing in place of one's real father and who becomes the object of emotions aroused by the original. More generally an older person, usually in a position of authority, with whom one identifies and to whom one looks for fatherly advice and approval.

fear of failure   Aroused when a person feels pressured to achieve and particularly prevalent in people with a high NEED FOR ACHIEVEMENT.

fear of success   Has been used mainly to describe a motive in some women to avoid doing well and achieving success (especially in competition with men) because their SOCIALISATION has led them to perceive such behaviour as unfeminine. Now thought to be relevant to men also. Difficult to distinguish sometimes from FEAR OF FAILURE.

Fechner's law   Named after the German physicist and psychologist Gustav Fechner. Large increases in the intensity of a stimulus produce smaller, proportional increases in the intensity perceived. It is expressed mathematically as $S = k \log R$, where S is the intensity experienced, R is the actual physical intensity, and k is a constant. This is one of the first attempts at a mathematical statement of a psychological phenomenon. It grew out of the studies in PSYCHOPHYSICS with which psychology became an experimental science in the 1870s.

feedback   A term borrowed from CYBERNETICS where it refers to the direct relationship of the input of a system to its output. The concept of a return flow of output information that can be used to regulate future input is now widely used in PROGRAMMED LEARNING and the development of TEACHING MACHINES.

feeling tone   The pleasantness or unpleasantness of the sensation one experiences from the stimulus of a given person, object, or situation.

feminism   A social movement or a viewpoint committed to the removal of PREJUDICE against women, differential treatment of men and women, and to the advancement of women's interests in general.

feral child   A child supposedly reared by animals in the wild. Such tales are part of the folklore of pop psychology and should be taken with a pinch of salt.

fetishism   In ANTHROPOLOGY, the worship of a fetish or inanimate object that is believed to possess magical powers. The term has been taken over by CLINICAL PSYCHOLOGY to refer mainly to the sexual excitement in men produced by an object associated with women. Favourite fetishes are hair, feet, shoes, underwear, and those black silk stockings with the little red bits at the top.

field   This term is sometimes used to denote all the interdependent factors in an organism's environment leading up to a particular piece of behaviour.

field dependence   A perceptual style in which PERCEPTION is distorted by background or contextual factors.

field experiment   A study in which the experimental method is used in a more naturalistic situation.

field theory   In its best known form, the school of GESTALT PSYCHOLOGY argued that in the functioning of the BRAIN and in the behaviour of people and the higher animals the whole is greater than the sum of all its parts, that the brain could be understood better as a total FIELD than as a collection of nerve cells, and that the cause of a particular piece of behaviour lies in the totality of a field of interacting elements rather than in the most obvious stimulus. In its social applications, field theory is closely linked to the work of KURT LEWIN.

field work Any study of human or animal behaviour outside of a laboratory or an EXPERIMENT.

fight-or-flight response In zoology, the choices an animal has built into its behavioural repertoire when faced with an intruder to its territory. The term is also used of human behaviour in the face of threat although it is more often misused to over-simplify behaviour that is far more complex than any animal behaviour. Inability to engage in either fight or flight is a frequent trigger for STRESS.

figural after-effect The perceptual distortion that appears when a second pattern is looked at after a first that is different. The same relationships between FIGURE-AND-GROUND that were seen in the first pattern tend to be perceived in the second.

figure-and-ground Apparently one of the psychological pre-requisites for PERCEPTION to take place is that the perceptual field is organised as figures distinguished against a relatively homogeneous background. Figure is usually the part of the field that is attended to, although the relationship between figure and ground can switch. The whole phenomenon is best illustrated in an unusual perceptual field like an AMBIGUOUS FIGURE. (See Figure 1.)

fixation In FREUD's theory, spending a long time at a given stage of development because of problems or excessive gratification.

fixed action pattern More recent term for INSTINCT. Used of stereotypical behaviour that is not learned.

fixed-alternative Test or questionnaire items that require an answer from a given selection of alternatives.

flashbulb memory A long-lasting and vivid MEMORY of a specific event and the context in which it occurred. The event is important and emotionally significant (e.g., a national or personal event). The term "flashbulb" refers to the fact that it is as if a photographic image of the event and setting has been encoded, as the memory is so detailed and accurate. Examples include the atrocities of 11 September 2001, and the deaths of Princess Diana and John F. Kennedy.

flattening of affect Weakness or absence of emotional response when a strong response would be appropriate.

flicker fusion frequency See CRITICAL FLICKER FREQUENCY.

flight into illness Used in CLINICAL PSYCHOLOGY to describe someone who develops symptoms of illness as a way of escaping conflict. Some social scientists consider this the basis for a great deal of mental illness, especially among poor people living in deprived areas.

floating affect In PSYCHOANALYSIS, feelings that have become detached from their usual object and are then capable of being attached to another object.

flooding A form of BEHAVIOURAL THERAPY where a patient is given maximum exposure to a feared stimulus until their fear subsides, thus extinguishing a learned response.

folie à deux French term meaning "insanity of two" referring to a delusion shared by two people, who usually live together.

foraging The various actions performed by animals in their attempts to find suitable food.

forced-choice technique A situation where a subject is forced to choose one of a given series of judgements even though none of them may seem to be appropriate.

foreclosure An IDENTITY status during ADOLESCENCE in which the individual has not focused on identity issues, but has nevertheless made definite future commitments.

forensic psychology The study of the psychological factors involved in legal issues such as criminal behaviour, decision making by juries, and EYEWITNESS TESTIMONY.

forgetting The inability to recall or recognise information. Forgetting may occur because the information no longer exists in MEMORY and so is not available for retrieval or because it cannot be found and so is not accessible. Forgetting is more likely with information that needs to be recalled, as RECOGNITION is generally greater than RECALL.

formal operations The final stage in PIAGET's theory of COGNITIVE DEVELOPMENT, from 11 onwards. Thinking now involves formal internally consistent adult logic and abstract thinking.

forward conditioning A situation in which the CONDITIONED STIMULUS is presented a short time before the UNCONDITIONED STIMULUS, and remains while the unconditioned stimulus is presented.

framing effect Influence on decision produced by the phrasing or frame of a problem.

fraternal twins See DIZYGOTIC TWINS.

free association A method used in PSYCHOANALYSIS to access the UNCONSCIOUS MIND by asking the client to say the first thing that comes into his or her mind. Eventually from the patient's associations the analyst may start to perceive clues about areas of conflict and disturbances that are surfacing from the unconscious.

free-floating anxiety A chronic state of irrational ANXIETY that cannot be pinned down to any specific source but can attach itself to anything and everything.

free will The notion that we are free to make decisions.

frequency Either the number of cycles per second of a light or sound wave, or the number of times something occurs in a study.

frequency distribution A tabulation of the number of times something occurs in a study.

frequency polygon A graph showing the frequencies with which different scores are obtained by participants in a study.

Freud, Sigmund (1856–1939) Freud's work may be divided into three areas; his invention of PSYCHOANALYSIS as a therapeutic technique, his theory of PERSONALITY, and his social philosophy. The origins of Freud's ideas are more overtly personal than those of any other psychologist; it was an attempt to understand himself that led to the development of psychoanalysis. His father's death brought dreams that troubled him and in trying to make sense of them he found the way through to his own UNCONSCIOUS and his unresolved ambivalent feelings about his father—and about the Jewishness his father represented. The result was his first major work, *The Interpretation of Dreams*, widely regarded as his most original and influential book and the springboard for the rest of his thought.

Freudian slip A slip of the tongue, which FREUD, who denied the existence of randomness or accident in the way a person behaves, interpreted as a clue from the UNCONSCIOUS about a repressed conflict. See also PARAPRAXIS.

frustration–aggression hypothesis In SOCIAL PSYCHOLOGY, an explanation for aggressive behaviour that states that frustration always leads to aggression and aggression is always caused by frustration.

fugue From the Latin word for "flight", a fugue is a relatively long period of AMNESIA in which a person leaves his or her home, forgets their past, and goes off to start a new and very different life somewhere else. When the UNCONSCIOUS conflict underlying the amnesia has been dealt with the person will remember his or her old life and IDENTITY and forget the period of the fugue.

functional autonomy The concept, suggested by Gordon Allport, that a particular behaviour, which was originally engaged in to achieve a certain goal, may itself become a goal. This idea may be relevant in examples of EXTRINSIC MOTIVATION becoming INTRINSIC. For example a child who practises the violin because his parents won't love him or give him any pocket money if he doesn't, may come to enjoy the activity of playing the violin for its own sake (and even grow up to be a concert musician).

functional disorder Emotional disturbance that cannot be attributed to a physical cause. As a rule of thumb such disturbances are considered NEUROSES and physically based disorders are considered PSYCHOSES, but this is a gross over-simplification of a very complex problem about which very little is known.

functional fixedness The tendency to solve problems in a particular or fixed way.

functionalism A school of psychology that emphasises the *functions* or activities of the MIND rather than its content, which is the emphasis of its rival, STRUCTURALISM.

functional MRI (fMRI) Using the MRI technology to study the BRAIN in action.

fundamental attribution error The tendency when trying to identify the causes of a person's behaviour to overestimate the role of his or her personal characteristics and to underestimate the role of the situation.

G

gain–loss theory of interpersonal attraction An attempt to formulate a theory that takes account of changes in people's liking for each other. It suggests that increases or decreases in the rewarding behaviour we receive from another person have more effect on us than a constant level of liking or disliking. Thus we like best someone who starts out negatively in our estimation and becomes more positive, and we like least a person who starts out positive and becomes negative.

Gallup poll The first and the best-known technique for the mass sampling of public opinion; invented by the American social scientist George Gallup.

Galton, Francis (1822–1911) Cousin and disciple of CHARLES

DARWIN, who pioneered the testing of individual differences in mental abilities.

galvanic skin response   At times of emotional activity, electrical reactions can be detected by electrodes on the surface of the skin. The CORRELATION between the two forms the basis for a lie detector test, although like all correlations one is still left guessing as to what it actually means.

game theory   A mathematical approach to the study of conflict and decision making which treats conflict situations as though they were games with set tactics and strategies and totally rational players. Some of the simpler situations studied, like the PRISONER's DILEMMA, have been of interest to SOCIAL PSYCHOLOGISTS for models that would generate ideas about social behaviour.

gatekeeping   In SOCIOLOGY, the term for the process by which people are selected into, or kept out of, the elite circles of a society. Sometimes used of the flow of information into group decision making, as in GROUPTHINK.

Gaussian curve   The bell-shaped curve of a NORMAL DISTRIBUTION, named after Carl Gauss, a 19th-century German mathematician.

gender   The psychological characteristics associated with being male or female, i.e., masculinity and femininity.

gender bias   The differential treatment or representation of men and women based on STEREOTYPES rather than real differences.

gender identity   One's concept of being male or female, a fundamental part of the SELF-CONCEPT.

gender role   Those behaviours, attitudes, and interests that are considered appropriate for one gender and not the other.

gender schema   Organised set of beliefs about gender behaviour.

gender stereotypes   The social perception of a man or a woman based on beliefs about gender roles.

gene pool   The whole stock of different GENES in a breeding population of any species.

general adaptation syndrome (GAS)   The body's non-specific response to STRESS that consists of three stages: the alarm reaction, when the body responds with the heightened physiological reactivity of the FIGHT-OR-FLIGHT RESPONSE to meet the demands of the STRESSOR; resistance, when the body tries to cope with the stressor and outwardly appears to have returned to normal but inwardly is releasing high levels of stress hormones; and exhaustion, where resources are depleted and the body's defence against disease and illness is decreased.

generalisation The tendency of a CONDITIONED RESPONSE to occur in a weaker form to stimuli similar to the CONDITIONED STIMULUS.

generalised other According to the American sociologist G. H. Mead, the concept an individual has of how other people expect him or her to behave in a given situation. Compare with SIGNIFICANT OTHER.

General Problem Solver (GPS) A computer program devised by Newell and Simon based on MEANS–ENDS ANALYSIS.

generation gap Differences between parents and children in attitudes, beliefs, opinions, and values that are attributed at least in part to the effects of being socialised at different times; used to explain conflict between young people and older people. As generation gaps have been evident since the world began there may well be something to this, although the gap may be more apparent than real. See also COHORT EFFECT, SOCIALISATION, and ZEITGEIST.

generativity The task of ERIKSON's seventh stage of development to be achieved in middle age. It entails the ability to do creative work or be a creative parent.

genes Units of inheritance that form part of a CHROMOSOME. Some characteristics are determined by one gene whereas for others many genes are involved.

genetic determinism The view that animal behaviour is caused by genetic influences, this view underpins evolutionary explanations.

genetics The science of HEREDITY.

genital stage In PSYCHOANALYSIS, the mature state of psychosexual development where the individual is capable of a loving, fully sexual relationship. To achieve this stage one must successfully avoid being fixated at one of the earlier ORAL, ANAL, or PHALLIC stages.

genome The total genetic material of an individual organism.

genotype An individual's genetic potential. Compare with PHENOTYPE.

geons In Biederman's theory, the basic three-dimensional shapes that combine to form patterns, shapes, and objects.

gerontology The study of old age and the processes of AGEING.

Gesell development norms A pioneering attempt, by the

American psychologist Arnold Gesell, to produce a timetable for the usual appearance of physical abilities in infants and young children.

Gestalt A German word meaning a form, a configuration, or a whole, which has properties that are more than just the sum of its parts.

Gestalt completion test Incomplete pictures that can only be completed correctly if the subject perceives the underlying unity and wholeness of the picture.

Gestalt psychology A school of psychology that began in the early part of the 20th century as a reaction against the behavioural psychology of PAVLOV and WATSON, and insisted that psychological phenomena should be treated as *gestalten* which could not be equated with the elements that comprised them. The first gestalt psychologists, Kofka, KOHLER, and Wertheimer, arrived at their ideas after studies of PERCEPTION; they were struck by the way the BRAIN organised dots of light into visual patterns, or musical notes into melodies. Kohler later branched out into studies of INSIGHT LEARNING (see the AHA REACTION) in apes, and later Gestaltists like Goldstein and LEWIN have extended Gestalt ideas into areas of PERSONALITY and SOCIAL PSYCHOLOGY. Gestalt thinking on perception is now largely accepted by psychologists, and its approach is very much in tune with the COGNITIVE REVOLUTION, although some people would argue that there are areas of human behaviour that can still best be understood by an analysis of the elements involved.

glossolalia "Speaking in tongues"; babbling in what sounds like an unknown language (but isn't). Associated mainly with religious ecstasy but also found in people who are emotionally very disturbed.

glucostats Specialised NEURONS in the BRAIN and liver that measure the level of blood glucose.

goal-directed behaviour Animal behaviour that can only be understood by assuming that it is intended to achieve a particular goal.

goal-setting theory A theory that suggests that MOTIVATION is raised by setting appropriate long-term incentives or goals.

Goodenough Draw-a-Person Test An INTELLIGENCE TEST for children under the age of 12, invented by the American psychologist Florence Goodenough, where the subject is asked to draw a picture of a person. About as culture-free as such a test can be.

gradient A constant rate of change between two conditions or VARIABLES.

grand mal See EPILEPSY.

graphology The use of handwriting as a kind of PROJECTIVE TECHNIQUE where a person's handwriting is analysed for whatever it may reveal about his or her PERSONALITY.

grasping reflex The automatic response by fingers or toes in infants when the palm or the sole of the foot is stimulated.

great-man theory The idea that the course of events is influenced at crucial times by the actions of outstanding individuals. As a way of understanding history it is a gross over-simplification.

group dynamics The study of the way people behave in groups, especially small or FACE-TO-FACE GROUPS. Associated with the pioneering work of KURT LEWIN.

grouping The statistical process of combining individual scores into categories or ranking them as, for example, PERCENTILES.

group mind A hypothetical entity, sometimes given mystical qualities, which has been suggested as the agency for crowds acting in unison. It is a way of saying we don't understand very much about crowd behaviour. Compare with COLLECTIVE MIND.

group norm Behaviour expected of all the members of a group. See NORM.

group polarisation The tendency of a group to become more extreme in its decision making than its individual members. Thus cautious individuals will spark an even more CAUTIOUS SHIFT and risk-taking individuals a more RISKY SHIFT.

group selection theory The notion that, if a group of animals possess more favourable characteristics, the group will be more likely to survive to reproduce.

group socialisation theory The view that children are socialised by groups outside the home, especially their PEER GROUPS, rather than the family.

group-splitting hypothesis An account of SCHIZOPHRENIA in which the individual thought to be schizophrenic seems to act in a manner similar to a leader splitting up a group that has become too large to function well.

group test A PAPER-AND-PENCIL TEST given simultaneously to a large group of people.

group therapy PSYCHOTHERAPY involving several people at the

71

same time. The assumption is that people can benefit from the experiences and companionship of other people.

groupthink   Excessive CONFORMITY to group opinion which can result in a group deciding on a highly inappropriate course of action or rejecting eminently sensible ideas. Originally George Orwell's term for the totalitarian imposition of authorised thoughts on all the members of a society.

GSR   See GALVANIC SKIN RESPONSE.

guiding fiction   A concept, proposed by ALFRED ADLER, that people have constant principles by which they evaluate their experiences and behaviour. These guiding fictions form the background of people's lives and often unconsciously influence the basic elements of their character.

guilt   The awareness of having violated a social NORM of behaviour one identifies with, and feeling regret as a result. In PSYCHOANALYSIS guilt is the result of unconscious conflict where the SUPEREGO predominates and produces symptoms of NEUROSIS if the conflict is unresolved.

guilt culture   A CULTURE that relies on its members' consciences and feelings of GUILT to maintain order and social control. Such a culture is vulnerable to the ANTI-SOCIAL PERSONALITY, a person incapable of feeling guilt. Contrast with SHAME CULTURE.

H

habit   A learned response to a given situation which occurs in such a regular fashion that it appears to be virtually automatic—so it may even be mistaken for INNATE behaviour and considered an INSTINCT.

habituation   In EXPERIMENTAL PSYCHOLOGY, decreasing response to a stimulus as it becomes more familiar through repeated presentation. With reference to drug use, habituation is the condition, resulting from repeated use of a drug, where there is a psychological (though not a physical) dependence on the drug but with little or no desire to increase the dose.

hallucination   A perceptual illusion of a vivid experience that has no apparent reality in the external world. Usually associated with

PSYCHOSIS, although it can happen to anyone. Can also be drug-induced by the use of HALLUCINOGENS or PSYCHEDELIC drugs.

hallucinogen A drug, like LSD or mescaline, that induces HALLUCINATION.

halo effect The tendency for one outstanding TRAIT to unduly influence an overall impression. Compare with HORN EFFECT.

handedness An individual's preference to use one hand or side of the body for certain activities, such as writing or throwing a ball.

handicapping theory According to this theory in SOCIOBIOLOGY females select males who have a handicap because this suggests the male must be genetically robust to flourish despite its existence. Symmetry may be a handicap because of its physiological cost.

handwriting analysis See GRAPHOLOGY.

haplodiploidy A mechanism for sex determination found in some species of insects, in which males are derived from unfertilised eggs, whereas females are derived from fertilised eggs.

hardiness A cluster of TRAITS possessed by those people best able to cope with STRESS.

Hawthorne effect The changes that take place to participants' behaviour as a result of knowing they are being observed. A study was carried out at the Hawthorne works of the Western Electric Company in Illinois in the 1920s. Various attempts by the management to improve workers' conditions were made; they included changes in lighting, rest breaks, hours of work, and systems of payment. Each of these changes resulted in an increase in productivity—and so did a return to the original conditions of work. The investigators concluded that the changes in the external environment had not influenced the workers' performance so much as their PERCEPTION that people were interested in them and their work. An example of SOCIAL FACILITATION.

hearing loss The degeneration of an individual's hearing ability. Apart from physical damage or disease it is caused by prolonged exposure to noise (Figure 11).

hebephrenia One of the common forms of psychological disturbance classified as SCHIZOPHRENIA. It is characterised by giggling and silliness and displays of inappropriate emotions.

hedonic Relating to pleasure or the dimensions of pleasure versus pain.

hedonism In PSYCHOLOGY, the idea that all of our behaviour is

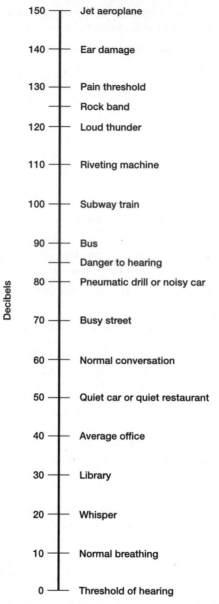

Figure 11 Hearing loss and the loudness of some familiar sounds

motivated by a need to pursue pleasure and avoid pain; in philosophy, the doctrine that it is our ethical duty to do so. The one does not imply the other.

hello–goodbye effect   The observation that patients tend to exaggerate their unhappiness at the beginning of therapy in order to convince the therapist that they are in genuine need. In contrast, at the end of therapy the reverse may be true; the patient may exaggerate their well-being to show appreciation to the therapist.

helplessness, learned   See LEARNED HELPLESSNESS.

hemispheres   The two halves of the forebrain or CEREBRUM.

hemispheric asymmetry   An imbalance between the two CEREBRAL HEMISPHERES, where one is dominant for some behaviour.

heredity   The biological transmission of characteristics from parents to offspring.

heritability estimate   An estimate of the importance of genetic factors which takes account of total variability in the population. It is calculated by working out the ratio between the genetic variability of the particular TRAIT and total variability in the whole population.

heritage   Everything transmitted from one generation to another, whether individually by HEREDITY or socially by custom, language, religion, and tradition, and physical possessions.

hermaphrodite   A person or animal with both male and female sex organs.

heteronomous morality   Younger children base their judgements of right and wrong on the severity of outcome and/or externally imposed rules.

heterosexual bias   The notion that HETEROSEXUALITY is more natural than, and preferable to, HOMOSEXUALITY.

heterosexuality   Being attracted by the opposite sex; the NORM in most societies and generally considered to be psychologically normal as well, although the implication that any other kind of sexuality is therefore ABNORMAL is now thought to be a dubious and over-simplified proposition.

heuristics   General guidelines or "rules of thumb" that may assist in problem solving or COGNITION generally, but do not guarantee a solution. Compare with ALGORITHMS.

hidden figure   See EMBEDDED FIGURE.

hidden observer phenomenon   In HYPNOSIS, a part of

consciousness that is separate from the hypnotised self and remains more aware of what is happening.

hierarchical model   A model where elements are organised in a hierarchy, suggesting some elements are more important/more developed or superior to others.

hierarchy of needs   In MASLOW's theory, a range of needs starting from physiological ones at the bottom of the hierarchy to SELF-ACTUALISATION at the top.

higher mental functions   According to Vygotsky those mental abilities, such as problem solving, that develop from elementary mental functions largely as a consequence of cultural influences.

higher-order conditioning   A technique used in CLASSICAL CONDITIONING in which a previously established CONDITIONED STIMULUS serves as the UNCONDITIONED STIMULUS for a new EXPERIMENT.

hindsight bias   The tendency to believe that we knew all along what the outcome of an event would be.

histogram   A graph in which the frequencies of scores in each category are represented by a vertical column; data on the y-axis must be continuous with a true zero.

holistic   Relating to the basic tenet of GESTALT PSYCHOLOGY that behaviour cannot be explained by reducing it to its simplest units.

holophrastic period   The first stage of language acquisition when children use holophrases—single words that express relatively complex meanings.

homeostasis   The process of maintaining a reasonably constant internal environment. See also SERVOMECHANISM.

homeostatic drive theory   An explanation of MOTIVATION that proposes that animals are motivated to seek food or liquid in order to return their body to a steady state. Once this occurs the drive is reduced.

homing   Behaviour used by an animal to locate, for example, its home, point of origin, or food store.

homologous   Anatomical term for organs with similar origins in different species (like a human arm and a fish's fin) but which may have different functions.

homophobia   Literally, a PHOBIA about men; used of apparently heterosexual men who are threatened by overt male HOMOSEXUALITY.

homosexuality   Being attracted to people of the same sex. Contrast with HETEROSEXUALITY. See also LESBIANISM.

horizontal décalage PIAGET's concept that, at any stage of COGNI-TIVE DEVELOPMENT, not all aspects of the stage will appear at the same time.

horizontal–vertical illusion An optical illusion in which a vertical line appears to be longer than a horizontal line of equal length.

hormones Chemical substances produced by endocrine glands, and circulated in the blood. They only affect target organs and are produced in large quantities but disappear very quickly.

horn effect In SOCIAL PSYCHOLOGY the tendency to make a gener-alisation in judging a person from one negative characteristic to a total impression. (The "horn" is associated with the Devil.) A nega-tive form of HALO EFFECT.

horopter When both eyes are fixated on the same point, the horopter is the locus of all the points in the external world whose images stimulate corresponding points on both retinas and are thus perceived as single images.

"hot house" children Children whose intellectual capabilities have been artificially "ripened" through intensive instruction or stimulation.

human communication The exchange of information between people by any means, whether verbal (in speech and writing) or non verbal. The study of this field involves contributions from psychology, social science, computer science, logic, and linguistics. See NON-VERBAL COMMUNICATION.

human engineering See ERGONOMICS.

human factors See ERGONOMICS.

humanism A view of humanity based on shared belief in human worth, without reference to a "divine being" or god.

humanistic model A model of ABNORMALITY based on the humanistic approach that emphasises the uniqueness of each indi-vidual, a focus on the present rather than the past, the importance of subjective experience, and the drive of each individual to be self-righting and to SELF-ACTUALISE.

humanistic psychology A school of psychology that emphasises the qualities that differentiate human beings from other animals, particularly creativity, humour, play, and psychological growth in general. Sometimes called the "THIRD FORCE" as opposed to BEHAVIOURISM and PSYCHOANALYSIS. Its leading proponents are Gordon Allport, ABRAHAM MASLOW and CARL ROGERS.

Huntington's chorea An inherited progressively degenerative disease of the nervous system.

hydrocephalus Excessive amount of cerebrospinal fluid within the skull resulting in an enlarged skull and underdeveloped BRAIN.

hydrophobia Medical term for a symptom in humans of the disease rabies, meaning literally "fear of water". The fear in this case is not *psychologically* abnormal but a symptom of the disease.

hyperthyroidism Excessive secretions by the thyroid gland that seem to cause heightened activity and excitement.

hypnogenic Anything that helps to induce a state of HYPNOSIS.

hypnogogic state A state sometimes experienced during the first stage of sleep, accompanied by hallucinatory images.

hypnosis An induced condition of extreme suggestibility to the hypnotist. The typical hypnotic trance looks like sleep but is probably a very different state—the EEGs of people in hypnosis are apparently different from patterns associated with sleep. Despite the long history of interest in hypnosis not much is understood about it. But it is clearly a real and potentially powerful phenomenon. As far back as the mid-19th century two British surgeons, Braid and Esdaile, were performing successful battlefield surgery using hypnosis as a general anaesthetic. This development stopped with the invention of chloroform.

hypnotherapy The use of HYPNOSIS in PSYCHOTHERAPY.

hypochondria Neurotic concern for one's health.

hypothalamus The part of the BRAIN that integrates the activity of the AUTONOMIC NERVOUS SYSTEM. Involved with emotion, STRESS, MOTIVATION, and hunger.

hypothesis An explanation for observed data, which has still to be tested.

hypothetical construct A fiction or story put forward by a theorist to make sense of a phenomenon. An integral part of scientific advance, it applies equally to the term "atom" and the term "PERSONALITY".

hypothetico-deductive method The accepted method of conducting scientific investigations, first formulated by Galileo in the 17th century, in which a scientist observes something he or she doesn't understand, comes up with a tentative explanation or HYPOTHESIS from which a testable outcome can be deduced, and sees whether his or her predicted outcome is verified by observation.

hypovolemic thirst Thirst created by low blood volume.

hysteria From the Greek word for "womb" because it was originally thought that the emotional disturbances it described were exclusively female and caused by disorders of the womb. There is no general agreement on the symptoms of hysteria, although most authorities seem to regard DISSOCIATION as one defining characteristic. There are several recognised forms of hysteria, the most striking being CONVERSION HYSTERIA. PSYCHOANALYSIS regards all hysteria as NEUROSIS, the product of UNCONSCIOUS conflict. See BATTLE FATIGUE for a male form of hysteria.

hysterical paralysis See CONVERSION HYSTERIA.

I

iatrogenic Disorders that are produced by a physician or therapist unwittingly through selective attention and expectations. The term is also used more generally to include unexpected side-effects of accepted treatment.

iconic store The image of a visual stimulus that lasts for a second or two in the MEMORY. Compare with ECHOIC STORE.

id From the Latin word for "it"; according to FREUD the id houses the deepest UNCONSCIOUS drives which are most in touch with the biological nature of the body and is one of the three main aspects of the PERSONALITY. The id is dominated by the PLEASURE PRINCIPLE and causes problems for the EGO when its DRIVES are blocked.

ideal mental health A state of contentment that we all strive to achieve.

ideal self Holding certain values and standards for oneself (one's SELF) and striving to realise them.

idée fixe French for "fixed idea"; a persistent OBSESSION that is impervious to contradictory evidence or argument.

identical twins See MONOZYGOTIC TWINS.

identification Conforming to the demands of a given ROLE because of a desire to be like a particular person in that role.

identity Having essentially unchanging characteristics; the basic unity of a personality, especially the SELF-IMAGE.

identity achievement In adolescence an IDENTITY status in which the individual has focused on identity issues, and has made definite future commitments.

identity crisis   The state of lacking a clear sense of what one is; it is most common in ADOLESCENCE and early adulthood.

identity diffusion   An IDENTITY status in which the individual has not focused on identity issues and has made no definite future commitments.

identity formation   The task of ERIKSON's fifth stage of PERSONALITY development, in ADOLESCENCE, where the individual has to find his or her own personal IDENTITY.

idiographic approach   An approach that emphasises the uniqueness of the individual. Compare with NOMOTHETIC.

idiot savant   French for "scholarly idiot"; a person who appears to be mentally retarded but possesses outstanding mental abilities in one area. These abilities can include music, drawing, and—especially—computation.

illusion   A mistake in PERCEPTION either for physical reasons (an optical illusion like the MULLER-LYER illusion) or psychological reasons, as in HALLUCINATION.

illusion of outgroup homogeneity   The illusion that members of an OUTGROUP are more alike than they really are.

illusory correlation   The PERCEPTION of a relationship between things where none exists in reality.

imageless thought   A thought or sequence of thoughts with no accompanying image or sensation. Whether such thoughts exist has been debated since the time of the ancient Greeks; the weight of modern opinion among psychologists is that they do.

imago   In PSYCHOANALYSIS, an idealised representation of a person, usually a parent, which was formed in the UNCONSCIOUS during early childhood. The image remains the same into adulthood where it can have a powerful influence on behaviour, especially in providing MODELS for that person to fall in love with and become emotionally involved with in general.

imitation   In SOCIAL LEARNING THEORY, learning a complex set of behaviours from one's CONSPECIFICS.

immanent justice   Punishment should be fair; wrongdoing should always result in some punishment.

immune system   A system of cells (white blood cells) within the body that is concerned with fighting disease. The white blood cells, called leucocytes, include T and B cells and natural killer cells. They help prevent illness by fighting invading antigens such as viruses and bacteria.

implicit learning Complex learning that occurs without the learner being able to verbalise clearly what he or she has learned.

implicit memory Having a memory for previously learned activities (like riding a bike) or material (like poetry) that one apparently is not conscious of. Unlike EXPLICIT MEMORY it is often largely intact in people with AMNESIA.

implicit personality theory Generally the unquestioned assumptions an individual uses in thinking about the PERSONALITY of another person; specifically, the characteristics that tend to be associated with each other in judging someone's personality. For example, "warm" usually goes with "outgoing", "sociable", and "good-humoured"; "cold" with "withdrawn", "reserved", and "humourless". The concept is particularly associated with the American social psychologist Fritz Heider.

imposed etic The use of a technique developed in one culture to study another culture. See also ETHNOCENTRISM.

impression formation Forming a generalised judgement of a person by trying to make sense of the various bits of information we have about them. See also IMPRESSION MANAGEMENT.

impression management Associated with the Canadian sociologist Erving Goffman; the attempt to present oneself (one's SELF) to other people in such a way that they will react in a controllable or predictable fashion.

imprinting In ETHOLOGY, a form of LEARNING in very young animals at certain critical periods. The learning is rapid and usually irreversible. For instance some species of baby ducks will follow the first moving object they encounter after being hatched. This object, on which they are imprinted, is usually their mother but, as KONRAD LORENZ showed, it could just as easily be an ethologist. Imprinting is thus a useful biological mechanism, in an inflexible and limited kind of way, that includes most of the behaviour usually termed as instinctive.

inappropriate affect An emotional response that is grossly out of touch with the needs of the situation, e.g., laughing at a tragic event. Often regarded as a symptom of PSYCHOSIS.

incest Sexual intercourse between close relatives; how close and how related will vary from CULTURE to culture but apparently the taboo against it is universal.

incidental learning See LATENT LEARNING.

inclusive fitness Fitness that includes the reproductive success of one's genetic relatives, as such success is beneficial at the level of the GENES.

incongruence In ROGERS' approach, the discrepancies between an individual's SELF-CONCEPT and his or her IDEAL SELF.

incorrect comparison theory The notion that our PERCEPTION of visual ILLUSIONS is influenced by parts of the figure that are not being judged.

incremental learning Learning that takes place in a series of regular and orderly steps rather than following flashes of INSIGHT.

independent groups design A research design in which each participant is in one condition only. Each separate group of participants experiences different levels of the IV. Sometimes referred to as an unrelated or between-subjects design.

independent variable See IV.

indirect fitness Increasing one's own fitness through helping genetic relations to survive and reproduce.

individual differences The comparison of people's characteristics and performance, especially INTELLIGENCE and INTELLIGENCE TEST scores.

individualistic When used of a CULTURE, one that emphasises individuality, individual needs, and independence. People in individualistic cultures tend to live in small NUCLEAR FAMILIES. Contrast with COLLECTIVIST.

inductive reasoning The attempt to infer general principles from specific cases. Compare with DEDUCTIVE REASONING.

industrial psychology An earlier form of the term WORK PSYCHOLOGY, still widely used in the United States.

infantile amnesia Forgetting the memories of earliest childhood, explained by PSYCHOANALYSIS as REPRESSION. The non-existence of language with which to "fix" experience in the memory is also suggested as a cause, as is simply the immaturity of the nervous system.

infantile birth theories A young child's answer to the question "Where do babies come from?" The navel appears to be a firm favourite.

infantile sexuality   The concept that made FREUD a pariah to the Viennese medical establishment; the idea that infants can have sexual experiences, that the capacity to feel pleasure when the EROGENOUS ZONES are stimulated is present from birth.

infantilism   The condition of someone who has not developed psychologically beyond infancy or who regresses to that state when older.

inferential statistics   Procedures by which generalisations can be made from findings on representative samples to the larger groups from which they are drawn.

inferiority complex   According to ALFRED ADLER, an UNCONSCIOUS condition where the individual feels inadequate and resentful, often because of some physical feature regarded as a defect. This complex leads to distorted behaviours, the most striking of which is OVERCOMPENSATION for the perceived defect—a mechanism often invoked to explain aggressiveness in small men.

informational social influence   Yielding to group pressure because others are thought to possess more knowledge.

information processing   A key term in COGNITIVE PSYCHOLOGY used to denote what happens mentally between stimulus and response including PERCEPTION, MEMORY, thinking, problem solving, and decision making. Information is usually taken to be any stimulus with a mental content—an image, idea, fact, opinion, etc.

information-processing framework   An approach to understanding cognitive processes by making analogies with computing and information technology.

information theory   A study of the nature of information and the way it is communicated. It was originated by mathematicians and engineers and draws heavily on concepts from these fields but with advances in BRAIN research it has been used by psychologists and linguists.

informed consent   This is an ETHICAL GUIDELINE, which states that participants' agreement to take part in RESEARCH should be based on their full knowledge of the nature and purpose of the research. Thus they should be made aware of any tasks required of them and their right to withdraw, and any other aspects of the research that might affect their willingness to participate.

infradian rhythm   A biological rhythm that recurs in a cycle of more than 24 hours ("*infra*" and "*dies*" = below or lower frequency than a day); for example, the menstrual cycle.

83

ingroups The groups to which an individual belongs. Contrast with OUTGROUPS.

inhibition The blocking of one physiological or psychological process by another, e.g., the response to one sense receptor inhibiting response to another, or fear inhibiting escape from danger. In PSYCHOANALYSIS inhibition is used to describe an impulse from the ID being blocked from entering CONSCIOUSNESS by the SUPEREGO. This is not the same as REPRESSION where the impulse is actively held back.

inkblot test See RORSCHACH TEST.

innate A genetically inherited tendency that is present at birth although it may not become active until later life. Compare with CONGENITAL.

innate releasing mechanism A concept introduced by Nikolaas Tinbergen, a European pioneer of ETHOLOGY. His observations of stickleback fish led him to wonder how male sticklebacks, who never saw a female until they were sexually mature, knew to chase away certain sticklebacks (i.e., males) and to woo others (i.e., females). The fish were reacting to the presence of red colouring on the male's belly or its absence on the female's. This was the mechanism that released their innate response.

inner-directed A term introduced by David Riesman to describe people who react to pressures of social change on the basis of personal values internalised early in life. Contrast with OUTER-DIRECTED and TRADITION-DIRECTED.

inoculation In SOCIAL PSYCHOLOGY, a technique for strengthening a person's attitude and their resistance to persuasion by exposing them to a small dose of the opposing attitude.

insecure attachment The ATTACHMENT bond is weaker in insecure attachments and this may result in an anxious and insecure relationship between the infant and caregiver, such as AVOIDANT and RESISTANT ATTACHMENTS. Insecure attachments are assessed by the infant's separation distress, lack of STRANGER ANXIETY, and either avoidant or resistant reactions when reunited with the caregiver. The insecure attachment has a poor effect on development, as the infant has a negative working model of themselves and others.

insight In Freudian theory, access to and understanding of emotional memories emerging from the UNCONSCIOUS; the goal of therapy.

insight learning A form of learning first identified in GESTALT

PSYCHOLOGY, where a new behaviour is acquired simply through the sudden appearance of understanding, as in the AHA REACTION, rather than by TRIAL AND ERROR.

instinct An INNATE impulse or motive.

institutionalisation Used to describe both the act of committing someone to an institution, such as a mental hospital, and the state of an inmate of such a place who has adapted to it so thoroughly that he or she is incapable of living outside it.

institutional racism Racially prejudiced behaviour that has not been adopted consciously but is simply the consequence of conforming to the NORMS and conventions of a society whose institutions of law, government, education, and business systematically discriminate against particular racial groups.

instrumental aggression Harming another person in order to achieve some desired goal.

instrumental conditioning See OPERANT CONDITIONING.

instrumental learning See OPERANT CONDITIONING.

integration The process of organising different parts into a whole of a higher order; used widely in science, from the organisation of nervous impulses necessary for any kind of behaviour to the organisation of a whole society.

intellectualising Dealing with a situation solely in intellectual terms and ignoring or denying the emotion involved. In PSYCHO-ANALYSIS it is regarded as a form of DEFENCE MECHANISM to protect the EGO from unpleasant feelings.

intelligence Although psychologists have been discussing this concept since the 1870s there is no general agreement on what intelligence is. Most psychologists would probably agree that HEREDITY sets the limits of a person's intelligence and most would also agree that the ability to learn in one form or another (handling abstract ideas, adapting to new situations, perceiving complex relationships) is a sign of high intelligence—which doesn't get us very far but has never prevented psychologists from designing new intelligence tests. Intelligence is a good example of a PHENOTYPE.

intelligence quotient (IQ) A measure of general intellectual ability that can be calculated by dividing MENTAL AGE by chronological age.

intelligence test A test that is supposed to measure INTELLIGENCE. Its purpose is to discriminate between people who score high and people who score low (i.e., high and low IQ) for the purpose of assigning them to various educational, occupational, and social categories. High scores are supposed to denote high intelligence and vice versa, but in the absence of an agreed definition of intelligence the operational definition becomes circular—people score high on intelligence tests because they are highly intelligent because highly intelligent people score high on intelligence tests. There is also a great deal of evidence that intelligence tests tend to be biased in favour of white, urban, middle-class people in their selection of test items. See also BINET.

interaction process analysis A technique for recording and analysing the interactions between people in a FACE-TO-FACE GROUP.

inter-blob region The region around the BLOB in the VISUAL CORTEX that is sensitive to orientation, some movement, and BINOCULAR DISPARITY.

intercorrelations A table of CORRELATIONS between each and every one of a series of VARIABLES.

interference Two principal meanings in PSYCHOLOGY. (1) The change in PERCEPTION when two light or sound waves out of phase come together, and (2) more commonly where one kind of LEARNING inhibits or disturbs another.

inter-judge reliability As applied to diagnoses, the level of agreement on patients' diagnoses among different PSYCHIATRISTS or CLINICAL PSYCHOLOGISTS.

intermittent reinforcement In a CONDITIONING EXPERIMENT only intermittently rewarding an animal for making correct responses rather than continuously. Appears to produce slower but more strongly established conditioning.

internalisation Describes an individual adhering to the ideas, values, and behaviour of the majority because they accept and agree with their world view.

internal justification In SOCIAL PSYCHOLOGY, a way of resolving COGNITIVE DISSONANCE that underlies the most powerful kind of ATTITUDE change. For example, if you feel, on reflection, that you have an awful job you can resolve (psychologically) the dissonance between the cognitions "I am a sensible person" and "I choose to work in an awful job" either externally or internally. An external justification might be "I do it for the money", but that wouldn't change your opinion of the job. However if you began to consider the job in a different light and saw its more positive aspects you would be justifying your decision to work in an awful job internally. You would in fact be persuading *yourself.*

internal validity The VALIDITY of an EXPERIMENT in terms of the context in which it is carried out. Concerns events within the experiment as distinct from EXTERNAL VALIDITY.

International Classification of Diseases and Health Related Problems (ICD) A means of classifying mental disorders and providing basic health statistics, published by the World Health Organisation.

interpersonal attraction General term for an area of SOCIAL PSYCHOLOGY concerned with why people are attracted to each other. See GAIN–LOSS THEORY OF INTERPERSONAL ATTRACTION.

interposition A situation where one object is partially obscuring another to provide a background cue to the perception of distance.

intersexual selection Sexual selection based on the members of one sex (usually female) selecting or choosing opposite-sexed mates.

intersubjectivity A process by which two individuals with different views about a task adjust those views so they become more similar.

interval data Data measured using units of equal intervals; the intervals reflect a real difference.

intervening variable An inferred process of a hypothetical variable that is supposed to occur between a stimulus and a response. See BLACK BOX.

interview A verbal RESEARCH method in which the participant answers a series of questions.

interviewer bias The effects on an INTERVIEW of the conscious and unconscious biases (assumptions, expectations) of the interviewer. Sometimes extended to include the whole process from constructing the interview schedule to interpreting the data. See also EXPERIMENTER BIAS, ROSENTHAL EFFECT, and SELF-FULFILLING PROPHECY.

intrapsychic Refers to conflicts or processes that take place within the PSYCHE (i.e., the MIND, PERSONALITY or SELF).

intrasexual selection Sexual selection based on competition for mates among the same-sexed (generally male) members of a species.

intrinsic A feature of an organism that is inherent in it, i.e., internal.

intrinsic motivation Doing something for its own sake because the activity itself is rewarding. Always contrasted with EXTRINSIC MOTIVATION. See FUNCTIONAL AUTONOMY.

intropunitive Blaming and punishing oneself, or feeling guilty and humiliated, in response to frustration. Contrast with EXTRAPUNITIVE.

introspection Examination and observation of one's own mental processes.

introversion According to JUNG, a basic PERSONALITY dimension of being withdrawn, inward looking, and passive, which is usually contrasted with EXTRAVERSION.

invariants In Gibson's theory, those aspects of the visual environment that remain the same as an observer moves.

investigator effects The effects of an investigator's expectations on the response of a participant. Sometimes referred to as the experimenter expectancy effect. See EXPERIMENTER BIAS.

involution Literally the opposite of EVOLUTION, i.e., decline or deterioration; used of mid-life physical and psychological crises and changes. See INVOLUTIONAL MELANCHOLIA and MIDDLESCENCE.

involutional melancholia A state of DEPRESSION and ANXIETY associated traditionally with the menopause and with mid-life crises in general.

IQ See INTELLIGENCE QUOTIENT.

IRM See INNATE RELEASING MECHANISM.

irrational Something that is inconsistent with logic or reason.

Ishihara test A test for COLOUR BLINDNESS in which the subject has to pick out a pattern against a complex background of different colours. People with normal COLOUR VISION can perceive the pattern and colour blind people cannot.

item analysis A technique to determine the effectiveness of different items on a test for discriminating between the people who take it.

IV (independent variable) Some aspect of the RESEARCH situation that is manipulated by the researcher in order to observe whether a change occurs in another variable.

J

J curve A FREQUENCY DISTRIBUTION of conforming behaviour portraying on a graph that the behaviour of most people will fall at or near the behaviour expected. The curve looks roughly like a capital letter J, or a reverse J, in shape.

James–Lange theory of emotions A fusion of two similar theories of the emotions put forward by the American philosopher William James and the Danish physiologist C. G. Lange. In essence they suggest that what we refer to as emotion is our conscious awareness of the bodily changes that follow an exciting event. Thus it would be more correct to say that we are sad because we cry, rather than that we cry because we are sad. Contrast with BARD–CANNON THEORY.

jigsaw classroom An approach to reducing PREJUDICE in which the teacher makes sure that all of the children can contribute to the achievement of classroom goals.

jnd See JUST NOTICEABLE DIFFERENCE.

job analysis One of the key roles of work psychologists, where the elements of a job are studied in an attempt to match the tasks to be performed with the workers' abilities to perform them.

Jung, Carl Gustav (1875–1961) A Swiss PSYCHOANALYST and one of FREUD's earliest colleagues. For about 6 years they were very close and Freud regarded Jung as the heir apparent to the movement he had founded. Jung was a PSYCHIATRIST of some status and, importantly for Freud, a Christian, the son of a Protestant minister. Jung left the Freudian movement in 1914 and founded his own, largely because he could not accept Freud's uncompromising stand on the fundamental importance of sex in the origin of NEUROSIS. Jung's interests were also more mystically inclined than Freud's devotion to rationality could tolerate—Jung studied practically everything from alchemy to yoga. See especially ARCHETYPES and INTROVERSION–EXTRAVERSION.

just noticeable difference The minimum amount of difference that a subject can detect between two stimuli.

just-world hypothesis In SOCIAL PSYCHOLOGY, the term used for the unquestioned assumption that the world is a just place where the deserving are rewarded and the undeserving punished. It therefore follows that if people are punished they must have done something to deserve it, and this is how the hypothesis accounts for people who blame victims for their own misfortunes. See also DISTRIBUTIVE JUSTICE.

K

kin selection The view that the process of NATURAL SELECTION functions at the level of an individual's GENES and thus any behaviour that promotes the survival and reproduction of all "kin" (genetic relatives) will also be selected.

kinaesthetic Refers to the sense that deals with movement of the body and the limbs. See PROPRIOCEPTORS.

Kinsey report The first ever large-scale survey of human sexual behaviour, carried out in the United States in the 1940s and 1950s by Alfred Kinsey. Still regarded by some as an illuminating pioneer work despite heavy criticism of its methodology.

kinship system In ANTHROPOLOGY, the web of family relationships and the behaviour associated with them.

Klein, Melanie (1882–1960) A pioneer, especially influential in the United Kingdom, in the PSYCHOANALYSIS of children and of RESEARCH into DEPRESSION. Kleinians still consider themselves basically Freudian while differing on several major points of theory in the very early development of PERSONALITY.

kleptomania A COMPULSION to steal. See also MANIA.

Klüver–Bucy syndrome A pattern of behaviour associated with removal of, damage to, or tumours in the temporal lobe of the BRAIN leading to, e.g., reduced aggression and increased sexual behaviour.

Kohler, Wolfgang (1887–1967) One of the founders of GESTALT PSYCHOLOGY. His primary contribution was his work on INSIGHT LEARNING with apes during which he discovered the AHA REACTION.

Korsakoff's syndrome A MEMORY disorder involving AMNESIA, due mostly to alcoholism, first observed by the 19th-century Russian neurologist Sergei Korsakoff.

Kuder Preference Record A questionnaire designed to elicit a subject's areas of vocational interest, developed by the American psychologist George Kuder.

L

labelling theory   The notion that attaching a psychiatric label to a patient may worsen his or her condition, because he or she is then treated as someone who is mentally ill. See also SELF-FULFILLING PROPHECY.

labile   The free and swiftly changing expression of emotion.

laboratory experiment   An experiment conducted in a laboratory setting or other contrived setting away from the participants' normal environments. The experimenter is able to manipulate the IV and accurately measure the DV, and considerable control can be exercised over CONFOUNDING VARIABLES.

Laing, Ronald D. (1927–1989)   A Scottish psychiatrist whose comprehensive criticisms of traditional psychiatric diagnosis and treatment have been fairly influential. A leading figure in the EXISTENTIAL PSYCHIATRY movement. Laing was particularly concerned with the origins of emotional disturbance within the system of family relationships.

Lamarckianism   A theory of EVOLUTION proposed by the 19th-century French biologist Henri Lamarck and suggesting that an animal's ACQUIRED CHARACTERISTICS could be genetically transmitted to its offspring. Scientists have generally preferred DARWIN's rival theory of evolution.

language acquisition device   INNATE knowledge of grammatical structure, which is used to assist language LEARNING.

language codes   See ELABORATED CODE and RESTRICTED CODE.

latency period   In PSYCHOANALYSIS, the period between age 4 or 5 and the beginning of ADOLESCENCE when interest in sex is supposed to be either non-existent or sublimated.

latent content   In FREUD's theory, the underlying meaning of a dream. Compare with MANIFEST CONTENT.

latent learning   Learning that takes place in the absence of any observable behaviour, or with no apparent REINFORCEMENT.

lateral inhibition   A process in which the firing of RECEPTORS inhibits the firing of adjacent receptors, thus causing contrast enhancement.

lateralisation   The tendency for some neural functions to be

91

located in one CEREBRAL HEMISPHERE rather than the other, as in the case of language in the left hemisphere.

laterality Literally "sidedness"; preferring either the left hand or foot, for instance, for a task that can be accomplished with either left or right limb. See BILATERAL TRANSFER.

lateral thinking A term suggested by Edward De Bono to describe an attempt to solve a problem by looking at it from various angles rather than head-on, thus allowing the problem to be re-conceptualised and perhaps solved by a previously unacceptable or unthought-of solution. A form of HEURISTIC.

law of parsimony See OCCAM'S RAZOR.

law of reinforcement The probability of a given response being produced is increased if it is followed by reward or a positive reinforcer.

laws of association The principle underlying the connections in the MEMORY between certain ideas, feelings, or behaviours. Aristotle made the first formulation of these principles in the 4th century BC.

lay analyst The name given to a PSYCHOANALYST without a medical degree.

leadership A form of social influence where one member of a group alters the behaviour and/or thoughts of others with the aim of reaching a specific goal.

learned helplessness Passive behaviour produced by the PERCEPTION that punishment is unavoidable.

learning A relatively permanent change in behaviour, which is not due to MATURATION.

learning curve The curve obtained by plotting on a graph measured changes in learning performance over time.

learning plateau A flattening of the learning curve due to a temporary halt in learning progress.

learning set Sometimes described as "learning how to learn"; a generalised approach to problems in which animals or people carry over to a new learning situation the responses and strategies they learned in a previous situation. TRANSFER OF TRAINING results from a learning set.

learning styles The different approaches people take to the process of learning based on individual differences in COGNITION and PERSONALITY.

learning theory   An attempt to explain the process of LEARNING.

legitimate authority   The assumption that people in positions of power have earned the right to tell others what to do because they have superior expertise, knowledge, or ability.

lesbianism   Female HOMOSEXUALITY. The word "homosexual" can be applied to women because it is derived from the Greek "*homos*" (same) rather than the Latin "*homo*" (man). "Lesbian" is from the Greek island of Lesbos which in antiquity was associated with female homosexuality.

lesion   A wound or injury. When BRAIN lesions are produced surgically, the amount of tissue destroyed is typically less than with ABLATION.

level of aspiration   The goals or standards of performance people set for themselves.

levels of processing   The extent to which something is processed, not in terms of how much processing is done (as in repetition), but in terms of how much meaning is extracted. Shallow processing focuses on the superficial features of the information, such as whether a word is in upper or lower case, whilst deep processing focuses on the meaning of the information and is thought to lead to better retention.

levels of significance   See STATISTICAL SIGNIFICANCE.

Lewin, Kurt (1890–1947)   A student of the early GESTALT psychologists who applied some of their thinking to SOCIAL PSYCHOLOGY where he pioneered the field of GROUP DYNAMICS.

liberal humanism   The view that all people, e.g., gays, lesbians, and heterosexuals, are equal and that the ways they conduct relationships are basically similar.

libido   FREUD's term for the psychological energy that is associated with sexual DRIVES. At each stage of psychosexual development, the libido becomes focused on a part of the body.

lie detector   An instrument for monitoring physiological changes like heart rate and electrical resistance of the skin under conditions of emotional stress. The assumption is that the subject will show signs of emotional upheaval if he or she lies in answer to a question. It's a big assumption.

life changes   Life changes require some degree of social readjustment or alteration in the individual's current life patterns, which is the response to a significant life event. For example, death, divorce, a change of job, marriage, vacation, or Christmas. Each life event is assigned a life change unit (LCU) based on how much readjustment the change would necessitate. The ADAPTATION needed to cope with the life change absorbs energy, and so depletes the body's resources, and thus life changes are a source of STRESS.

life cycle   In Levinson's theory of adult development, the sequence of four different periods spanning adult life.

life events   Experiences that are common to most people and involve change from a steady state; they are a means of explaining why some people become ill.

life instinct   According to FREUD, an UNCONSCIOUS DRIVE, or set of drives, towards the preservation and enhancement of life, whose energy comes from the LIBIDO. Always contrasted with the DEATH INSTINCT.

life space   A term introduced by KURT LEWIN to describe the totality of the physical and psychological factors in the environment of an individual or group at any one time.

life structure   The underlying pattern of someone's life at a given time.

Likert scale   A technique developed by the American scientist Rensis Likert, for constructing ATTITUDE measures where the subject indicates on a three- or five-point scale whether he or she agrees or disagrees with a particular statement.

limbic model   A physiological account of EMOTION identifying the BRAIN structures involved (the LIMBIC SYSTEM).

limbic system   A group of BRAIN structures thought to be particularly important in the regulation of EMOTION and MOTIVATION. Part of the area sometimes known as the OLD BRAIN.

limen   See THRESHOLD.

linguistic determinism   The HYPOTHESIS that the possible thoughts available to people are shaped by their language.

linguistic relativity   See LINGUISTIC DETERMINISM.

Little Albert   The child conditioned by J. B. WATSON to fear rats.

Little Hans   A young patient whom FREUD cured of a PHOBIA about horses. Not to be confused with CLEVER HANS.

Lloyd Morgan's Canon   The principle in COMPARATIVE PSYCHOLOGY, suggested by the British psychologist Lloyd Morgan in 1894, that any interpretation of an animal's behaviour must be the simplest possible to account for what is observed. Thus an explanation requiring a higher psychological functioning should not be offered if a lower will suffice. A special case of OCCAM'S RAZOR.

lobotomy   A type of PSYCHOSURGERY, where the frontal lobes are severed from the main part of the BRAIN. Formerly used widely as a last resort for severe DEPRESSION but less common now.

localisation   The view that certain areas of the CEREBRAL CORTEX are associated with specific behavioural functions.

locus of control   A PERSONALITY dimension in which people who have an internal locus of control feel they have control over what happens to them, and people with an external locus of control tend to attribute their experiences to outside forces or other people.

longitudinal research   Repeated study of the same people over a period of time. Compare with CROSS-SECTIONAL RESEARCH and see also COHORT EFFECT.

long-term memory (LTM)   A relatively permanent store, which has unlimited capacity and duration. Different kinds of long-term memory have been identified, including EPISODIC (memory for personal events), SEMANTIC (memory for facts and information), and procedural (memory for actions and skills).

Lorenz, Konrad (1903–1989)   An Austrian pioneer of ETHOLOGY whose books *King Solomon's Ring* and *On Aggression* helped popularise the subject.

loss aversion   Greater sensitivity to losses than to gains.

LTM   See LONG-TERM MEMORY.

lucid dreams   A dream where the individual is aware that they are dreaming and can sometimes control the dream content.

M

MA   See MENTAL AGE.

Machiavellian intelligence   The capacity to intentionally deceive another individual.

machine reductionism   Explaining behaviour by analogy with rather simpler machine systems.

magic thinking   Any attempt to understand and manipulate the human condition by recourse to supernatural powers. In particular the term is used to describe the belief that there is a causal link between one's wishes and the real world, that "wishing can make it so". Said to be typical of children, psychotics, and pre-literate peoples.

mand This refers to a word that is learned because its meaning is of significance in the child's life.

mandala In JUNG's theories, a magic circle that represents the striving for total unity of the SELF. The idea comes from symbols of the cosmos found in different cultures.

mania Uncontrollable excitement accompanied by the impulse to perform a particular kind of behaviour.

manic Behaviour characterised by a MANIA.

manic-depressive A PSYCHOSIS typified by extreme swings of mood from the wild excitement of MANIA to the inadequacy and anxiety of deep DEPRESSION. In "normal" people the swings range from "being high" to "having the blues". See also BIPOLAR DISORDER.

manifest content In FREUD's theory, the actual or obvious content of a DREAM. Compare with LATENT CONTENT.

manipulation Where an animal is tricked or manipulated by another into behaving in an apparently altruistic way. An evolutionary explanation for what looks like altruism in animals.

mantra A word or phrase repeated over and over as an aid to meditation.

map–compass hypothesis The idea that navigation is achieved by using the sun as a compass in addition to knowledge of visual landmarks, which serve as a map. True navigation requires a map and a compass.

marasmus Severe physiological weakness found in infants suffering from a DEPRIVATION of either food or love.

marginality In SOCIAL SCIENCE, a term used to denote the effects on an individual or group of being excluded from the mainstream of a society.

masking The blocking of one sensory stimulus or process by another.

Maslow, Abraham (1908–1970) An American PERSONALITY theorist and leading exponent of HUMANISTIC PSYCHOLOGY, closely associated with the terms PEAK EXPERIENCE and SELF-ACTUALISATION.

masochism The experience of sexual pleasure through suffering physical pain. Usually considered a sexual perversion. Named after Sader Masoch, an exponent of the practice. In PSYCHOANALYSIS, masochism is seen as a form of turning one's destructive DRIVES inwards. Usually coupled with SADISM as SADO-MASOCHISM.

mass action The principle that the amount of material stored in the CEREBRAL CORTEX is equivalent to the space it occupies. Thus the more cortex you remove, the more severe will be the likely resulting damage.

massed practice A technique of learning in which the lessons or periods of practice follow each other without a break. A much less effective method of learning than DISTRIBUTED PRACTICE with which it is usually contrasted.

matched pairs (matched participants) design A research design that matches participants on a one-to-one basis rather than as a whole group.

matching hypothesis The notion that we are attracted to those who are about as physically attractive as we are.

maternal deprivation hypothesis The view, suggested by BOWLBY, that separation from the primary caregiver (maternal deprivation) leads to bond disruption and possibly the breaking of the ATTACHMENT bond. This has long-term effects on emotional development. Bowlby believed that once broken the attachment bond could not be fixed and so the damage would be permanent.

matriarchy A society or a social group run by women. Contrast with PATRIARCHY.

matrilineal Applied to a society or social group where descent or inheritance is traced through the female line. Contrast with PATRILINEAL.

maturation The processes of growth and development that are common to all the members of a species and appear regardless of individual heredity or environment. It is a concept that cuts right across the NATURE–NURTURE DEBATE.

maze A device for studying LEARNING in both animals and humans, ranging from a single T-junction with a choice of two pathways to a complex labyrinth.

McNaughten rules A mid-19th-century legal ruling that is still widely used in deciding whether a criminal defendant is insane and therefore not responsible for his or her actions. The ruling states that a person is criminally liable unless their reason was so defective that they did not realise the nature of their action or that it was wrong.

97

mean   An average worked out by dividing the total of participants' scores by the number of participants.

means–ends analysis   A HEURISTIC method of problem solving in which the difference between current and goal states is reduced using subgoals.

measures of central tendency   The three statistics that can be used as a central value to describe a group of numbers, the MEAN, the MEDIAN and the MODE.

median   The middle score out of all the participants' scores when data have been put into numerical order.

mediate   Sometimes used in psychology to describe an activity, often cognitive, that comes between a stimulus and a response.

medical model   A model of ABNORMALITY based on the medical approach to treating physical illness; the model assumes that all illnesses (physical and psychological) have an underlying bio-chemical or physiological basis.

medulla oblongata   Part of the reticular formation in the BRAIN; it is involved in the control of breathing, digestion, and swallowing.

megalomaniac   A person with a mania for himself (or herself), having a wildly exaggerated view of his or her own abilities and importance.

melancholia   A pathological extent of a melancholy mood, char-acterised by sadness and severe DEPRESSION. See INVOLUTIONAL MELANCHOLIA.

melatonin   A HORMONE produced by the PINEAL GLAND that increases sleepiness.

membership group   In SOCIAL PSYCHOLOGY, the group to which an individual belongs. Compare with REFERENCE GROUP.

memory   The mental processes used to encode, store, and retrieve information. ENCODING takes many forms; visual, auditory, seman-tic, taste, and smell. Storage refers to the amount of information that can be held in memory. Retrieval refers to the processes by which information is "dug out" of memory, and includes RECOGNI-TION, RECALL, and reconstruction. It is useful to distinguish between two types of memory: SHORT-TERM or immediate memory and LONG-TERM or more permanent memory.

memory for faces   This relies on the accurate recognition and recall of faces. FACE RECOGNITION seems to rely on a combination of factors such as the features, configuration (overall arrangement), and movements of the face. Identification of the criminal means memory for faces provides key information in EYEWITNESS TESTI-MONY. However, memory for faces is subject to the same distortions due to RECONSTRUCTIVE MEMORY and emotional factors as other types of MEMORY.

memory span   The number of items a subject can recall after a single presentation of material. See DIGIT-SPAN TEST.

memory trace   See ENGRAM.

Mendelian genetics   An explanation for the mechanisms of inheritance based on single GENES, named after Gregor Mendel.

mental age   A score on an INTELLIGENCE TEST where items are graded by difficulty and supposedly standardised against chrono-logical age. See INTELLIGENCE QUOTIENT.

mental defective   A vague general term used to describe a person who is considered to have insufficient mental development to cope with everyday life and needs special care. Now regarded by psycho-logists as unhelpful and offensive.

mental retardation   Technically used term in Britain and North America for describing people who score less than a 70 IQ.

mental set   An expectation of, or readiness for, a particular experience.

mere exposure   In SOCIAL PSYCHOLOGY, a term introduced by the American scientist Robert Zajonc to explain the phenomenon that, other things being equal, the more familiar people become with objects, words, or pictures they don't know, the more they like them. Mere exposure may thus help to explain the influence of advertising on buying habits.

Merrill–Palmer scale   A test of verbal and manipulative ability for young children.

mesmerism   An early name for HYPNOSIS, named after the 18th-century exponent, the Austrian physician Franz Mesmer (who called it animal magnetism).

meta-analysis   An analysis in which all of the findings from many studies relating to a given HYPOTHESIS are combined for statistical testing.

metacognitive knowledge   Knowledge about the usefulness of various cognitive processes relevant to LEARNING.

metapsychology   Used in two senses: either (1) an attempt to include the whole of psychology in one comprehensive theory, or (2) to go beyond existing theory and observations and speculate about the human condition in general.

methodological behaviourism   The view that all psychological perspectives use some behaviourist concepts to explain behaviour.

micro-environment   The view that each individual to a certain extent creates his or her own environment through their behaviour and physical characteristics.

micro-sleep   Brief periods of relaxed wakefulness during the day when a person stares blankly into space and temporarily loses awareness. Such periods may permit some restorative functions to take place.

middlescence   A term sometimes used in DEVELOPMENTAL PSYCHOLOGY to focus attention on the psychological STRESSES and conflict of the middle years of life, as well as the unique and positive aspects of this period.

migration   Travel over long distances to specific locations.

milieu therapy   A form of PSYCHOTHERAPY that focuses on helping people by changing their environment rather than their own ATTITUDES or behaviour.

Miller Analogies Test   An instrument, using difficult analogy problems, devised to predict future performance in applicants for graduate study at American universities.

mind   A vague term used for many centuries in many different ways. As used today by psychologists it most often refers to the totality of organised, mainly cognitive psychological processes.

mind–body problem   One of the most ancient of philosophical debates: What is the relationship of the mind to the body? Answers to this question have included: (1) They influence each other totally; (2) They don't influence each other at all; (3) Mind doesn't really exist; (4) Body doesn't really exist; (5) Mind and body are really the same thing. And you wondered what philosophers did for a living.

mind map   A technique developed in the 1970s by Tony Buzan to aid MEMORY, thinking, and creativity. It involves a pictorial form of note taking, radiating out from a central theme and making use of shape and colour.

minimax strategy   In GAME THEORY, the strategy of choosing to minimise loss rather than maximising gain.

Minnesota Multiphasic Personality Inventory   A paper-and-pencil test containing 550 statements which the subject responds to as being true or false about him/herself. The pattern of responses is intended to uncover certain PERSONALITY characteristics, particularly those associated with a tendency towards psychological disturbance.

minority influence A majority being influenced to accept the beliefs or behaviour of a minority. This usually involves a shift in private opinion, as the majority needs to accept the minority as "right" if they are to reject the dominant majority. This private change involves a process of conversion, which is more likely to occur when the minority is consistent and flexible, as this is more persuasive.

mirror test A test of self-recognition using a mirror, in which a red mark is put on an animal's face.

mirror writing Writing that is reversed but appears as normal when seen in a mirror. Sometimes found in people diagnosed as SCHIZOPHRENIC, but more commonly in children who have a problem with LATERALITY.

misanthropic Hating other people.

misapplied size-constancy theory A theory proposed by Gregory, according to which the processes producing size constancy with three-dimensional objects are used inappropriately in the perception of two-dimensional objects.

miscegenation Technically, breeding between two different genetic stocks. Used as a pejorative term for mixing of the "races', invariably black people with white people, whose differences are much more social than biological.

misogyny Hatred of women.

MMPI See MINNESOTA MULTIPHASIC PERSONALITY INVENTORY

mnemonics Tricks to aid the MEMORY.

modality Usually refers to a particular form of sensory experience, like vision or hearing.

modal personality Literally, the PERSONALITY that represents the mode of a group. A term in ANTHROPOLOGY for that hypothetical individual whose personality is typical and illustrative of a particular group or society.

mode The most frequently occurring score among participants' scores in a given condition.

model (1) A way of representing patterns of relationships observed in human behaviour. (2) In SOCIAL PSYCHOLOGY, a person whose behaviour is closely observed. See MODELLING.

modelling Imitation; a form of learning or therapy based on observing a model and imitating that behaviour.

molar Relating to something as a whole (e.g., swimming) rather than to its constituent parts (moving head, arms, and legs in certain ways). Contrast with MOLECULAR.

molecular Relating to the constituent parts of an activity (e.g., the head, arm, and leg movements in swimming) rather than the activity as a whole. Contrast with MOLAR.

monoamines A group of NEUROTRANSMITTERS that are chemically similar, such as SEROTONIN, dopamine, and NORADRENALINE. They are also called catecholamines.

monocular cues Cues to depth that only require the use of one eye.

monogamy A mating system in which a male and a female remain together over a long period, with both of them generally contributing to parental care.

monotropy hypothesis The notion that infants have an INNATE tendency to form strong bonds with one caregiver, usually their mother.

monozygotic twins Identical twins derived from the same fertilised ovum who therefore share 100% of their genes. Contrast with DIZYGOTIC TWINS.

mood-state-dependent memory Memory is better when the mood at the time of retrieval matches the mood at the time of learning.

moral development In DEVELOPMENTAL PSYCHOLOGY there is now a large measure of agreement that the ability to make moral judgements follows a sequence of stages like other aspects of development.

morality The principles used by individuals to distinguish between right and wrong.

moratorium An IDENTITY status in ADOLESCENCE in which the individual has focused on identity issues, but has made no definite future commitments.

Moro Reflex The startle response made by newborn infants, involving clutching movements of the arms and legs, first observed by the Austrian paediatrician Ernst Moro.

motherese A special style of speaking used by mothers when talking with children (also known as "parentese").

motion parallax A visual cue used to perceive motion and depth; things that are closer move faster in relation to things that are farther away.

motivation A general term for any part of the hypothetical psychological process that involves the experiencing of needs and DRIVES and the behaviour that leads to the goal which satisfies them.

motor Psychology term for muscular movement.

motor neuron A single nerve cell that activates a muscle or gland.

MRI scans Three-dimensional pictures of the BRAIN based on the detection of magnetic changes; MRI stands for magnetic resonance imaging.

Muller-Lyer illusion A distorted visual perception of length (see Figure 12). Named after the German psychologist Franz Muller-Lyer.

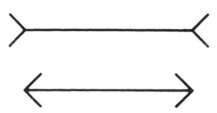

Figure 12 Muller-Lyer illusion. Both lines between the arrows are actually the same length

multimodal distribution A FREQUENCY DISTRIBUTION with several MODES.

multiple personality disorder See DISSOCIATIVE IDENTITY DISORDER.

multi-store model The concept that MEMORY is divided into several kinds of store (SENSORY, SHORT-TERM, and LONG-TERM). It is often assumed that attention is used to select some information from sensory memory for processing in the short-term store, whereas verbal rehearsal is involved when information is transferred from the short-term memory store to the long-term memory store. It is increasingly doubted that there is a single long-term memory store.

mundane realism The use of an artificial situation that closely resembles a natural situation.

Murphy's Law An Irish variant of SOD's LAW.

mutation A genetic change that can then be inherited by any offspring.

mutualism   Two individuals behaving in a co-operative or altruistic way towards each other at the same time.

N

N Ach   Abbreviation for NEED FOR ACHIEVEMENT

N Aff   Abbreviation for NEED FOR AFFILIATION

naïve participant   In psychology generally, a participant or subject who is unfamiliar with an EXPERIMENT; in SOCIAL PSYCHOLOGY, a participant who has been misled as to the real purpose of the experiment. For example, in studies of CONFORMITY it would be self-defeating to tell a participant that the point of the experiment was to see how far he or she would conform to group pressure, so the participant is given a cover story instead and debriefed about the real nature of the study when it is over.

narcissism   From the Greek myth of Narcissus who fell in love with his own reflection. Excessive self-love in whatever form, characterised by a preoccupation with oneself (one's SELF) to the exclusion of others. In PSYCHOANALYSIS, an early stage of psychosexual development where the self is the sexual object.

narcolepsy   A disease characterised by an uncontrollable need to sleep.

narcosis   A drug-induced stupor.

nativism   The view that people's characteristics are inherited.

natural experiment   A type of EXPERIMENT where use is made of some naturally occurring INDEPENDENT VARIABLE (IV); it is a quasi-experiment because the IV is not directly manipulated.

naturalistic observation   An unobtrusive observational study conducted in a natural setting.

natural selection   The process by which certain TRAITS (and the associated GENES) are perpetuated because of the advantage they confer in terms of survival and increased reproduction.

nature–nurture debate   The question of whether behaviour is determined by inherited factors or by experience (LEARNING). Now increasingly recognised as more than just an either/or question.

navigation   Using a compass and a "map" to find an exact location. A compass alone provides orientation.

necrophilia   A sexual attraction to dead bodies.

need for achievement   The strongly felt MOTIVATION to achieve, to accomplish ambitions, to be successful. It has been suggested that this motivation is inculcated by careful child-rearing patterns, particularly the fostering of early achievement by mothers in their first-born sons. Associated particularly with the American psychologist David McClelland.

need for affiliation   In SOCIAL PSYCHOLOGY, the need to be with other people, particularly when facing the same unpleasant experience. There is some evidence that this need may be related to birth order with last-born children having least need and first-born children (especially males) having most.

negative correlation   As one co-variable increases the other decreases. They still vary in a constant relationship.

negative reinforcement   Used in CONDITIONING for the rewarding of an act that ends an unpleasant state.

negative-state relief model   Cialdini *et al.*'s view that someone who feels empathy for a victim will help that person in order to relieve the sadness produced by the empathy.

negative transfer   The detrimental effect on later LEARNING of previous learning, because of the different responses required in the two situations. For instance, to steer a boat with a tiller after learning to drive a car. See TRANSFER OF TRAINING.

Neill, A. S. (1883–1976)   Scottish educator who founded a school in England called Summerhill with the goal of helping children lead lives free from REPRESSION. Although profoundly Freudian in its orientation, Neill's work has been claimed by HUMANISTIC psychologists and educators as an expression of their own principles.

neo-behaviourism   An extension of BEHAVIOURISM to allow for some cognitive factors, e.g., Bandura's SOCIAL LEARNING THEORY.

neo-dissociation theory   Hilgard's theory, according to which one part of the MIND is separated off from other parts in the hypnotic state.

neo-Freudian   A follower of FREUD who also accepts later modifications in psychoanalytic theory. Fromm, Horney, and Sullivan are the most prominent examples of such modifers. Early followers of Freud's who broke away from this movement, notably ADLER and JUNG, are usually known as *schismatics*.

neologism   Literally, a new word; sometimes found in SCHIZO-PHRENIC speech but more often in scientific and scholarly writing where common words are used in a new way, like CENSORSHIP and PROTOCOL, or where new words are concocted, like BRAINWASHING and TERRITORIALITY.

neonate   A newborn infant.

nervous breakdown   Popular term for a NEUROSIS severe enough to incapacitate an individual and require hospital treatment.

nesting instinct   The apparently INNATE activity of birds in building themselves a nest. Popularly supposed to apply to people as well, but that is an example of ANTHROPOMORPHISM and a gross over-simplification of human life.

neuroleptic drugs   Drugs that reduce psychotic symptoms but can produce some of the symptoms of neurological diseases.

neurology   The study of the structure and function of the nervous system.

neuron   The cell that constitutes the basic unit of the nervous system.

neurophysiology   The physiology of the nervous system.

neuropsychology   The aspects of PHYSIOLOGICAL PSYCHOLOGY concerned with the relationship between the nervous system, mental processes, and behaviour.

neurosis   A functional psychological disorder with no organic causes whose origins in emotional conflict can often be understood and dealt with by PSYCHOTHERAPY. Neurosis may be manifested as ANXIETY, FUGUE, HYSTERIA, OBSESSION, COMPULSION, or PHOBIA.

neurotic   Behaviour suggestive of NEUROSIS.

neurotransmitter   A chemical substance that is released at the junction between NEURONS (a SYNAPSE) and which affects the transmission of messages in the nervous system.

night blindness   A weakened capacity for DARK–LIGHT ADAPTATION due to organic disease or vitamin deficiency.

nominal data   Data consisting of the numbers of participants falling into qualitatively different categories.

nomothetic approach   An approach based on the attempt to establish general laws of behaviour. Compare with IDIOGRAPHIC.

nonconscious   ideology   The   unquestioned   assumptions people have about the world, which can influence their behaviour profoundly without their being aware of it.

non-directional (two-tailed) hypothesis A prediction that there will be a difference or CORRELATION between two VARIABLES, but no statement about the direction of the difference.

non-directive therapy A therapy that accepts an individual's expression of his or her needs and conflicts on that individual's own terms without any preconceived system of interpretation for steering the person in a particular direction. The most notable example of this kind of therapy is CARL ROGERS' CLIENT-CENTRED THERAPY.

non-mentalistic behaviour Behaviour involving no mental activity.

nonparametic statistics Statistical methods that may be used when the data do not conform to a NORMAL DISTRIBUTION, i.e., most data in studies of human behaviour.

nonsense syllables Three-letter combinations like ZEJ and TUZ that have no meaning for the participant (at least in English!) which are used in studies of MEMORY.

non-verbal communication Direct communication between people by means other than the spoken word; includes facial expressions, gestures, eye contact, and body posture.

noradrenaline One of the HORMONES (along with ADRENALINE) produced by the ADRENAL GLANDS which increases arousal by activating the sympathetic nervous system and reducing activity in the parasympathetic system.

norm (1) In statistics, a value representative of a whole group of numbers, such as one of the MEASURES OF CENTRAL TENDENCY (MEAN, MEDIAN, and MODE). (2) Cultural expectations, standards of behaviour. See also GROUP NORM and SOCIAL NORM.

normal Literally, conforming to the NORM or standard; as applied to behaviour it usually refers to what is expected (the SOCIAL NORM) or what is generally considered right, proper, or correct in the given circumstances.

normal distribution A bell-shaped distribution of data in which most of the scores are close to the MEAN. This characteristic shape is produced when measuring many psychological and biological variables, such as IQ and height (Figure 13).

normative social influence This occurs when someone conforms in order that others will like or respect him or her.

norm of reciprocity The cultural expectation that it is justified to treat others in the way they treat you.

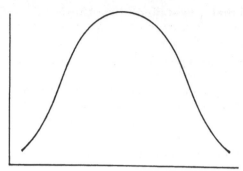

Figure 13 Normal distribution

norm of self-disclosure reciprocity The expectation that friends usually match how much they disclose about themselves, gradually increasing how much they mutually reveal.

norm of social responsibility The cultural expectation that help should be given to those in need of help.

nuclear family Mother, father, and 2.4 children. Contrast with EXTENDED FAMILY.

null hypothesis A HYPOTHESIS that states that any findings are due to chance factors and do not reflect a true difference, effect, or relationship.

nymphomaniac A woman with a MANIA for sex. See also SATYRIASIS.

nystagmus An involuntary and often repeated jerking of the eyes to one side followed by a slow return. It occurs normally after the head has been rotated but can also be a sign of BRAIN DAMAGE.

O

obedience to authority Behaving as instructed, usually in response to individual rather than group pressure. This usually takes place in a hierarchy where the person issuing the order is of higher status than the person obeying the order. Obedience occurs because the individual feels they have little choice; they cannot resist or refuse to obey. It is unlikely to involve a change in private opinion.

object blindness   See AGNOSIA.

object cathexis   Used in PSYCHOANALYSIS to signify the choice of a love object, usually involving the diversion of LIBIDO from a sexual to a non-sexual object. See also CATHEXIS.

object constancy   The way familiar objects are perceived in the same manner regardless of changes in the perceptual environment such as lighting, placement, and distance. See also COLOUR CONSTANCY.

objectification   Forming social representations by making abstract ideas more concrete.

objective   Dealing with facts in a way that is unaffected by feelings or opinions. Contrasted with SUBJECTIVE.

object libido   Used in PSYCHOANALYSIS, where LIBIDO is directed towards other objects rather than towards oneself as in NARCISSISM.

object loss   In PSYCHOANALYSIS, the loss of love from a valued external object.

object permanence   An awareness in young children that objects continue to exist when they can no longer be seen.

object-relations school   A group of British PSYCHOANALYSTS, including Ronald Fairbairn, MELANIE KLEIN, and Donald Winnicott who emphasised the importance of emotional relationships formed during the first 2 years of life. The "object" in question may be the infant's mother or its PERCEPTION and internal representation of the mother.

observational learning   A form of learning based on imitating or copying the behaviour of others.

observed value   The numerical value calculated when using a STATISTICAL TEST. The observed value is compared with the CRITICAL VALUE to determine significance.

obsession   A persistent ANXIETY-provoking idea that one can't seem to get rid of. Compare with COMPULSION.

obsessive-compulsive neurosis   A NEUROSIS in which an individual is not only obsessed by certain ideas but feels *compelled* to act on them, often ritually and repetitively, e.g., by counting windows or hand washing. In PSYCHOANALYSIS this behaviour is believed to be an effort to relieve guilt—as in the case of Lady Macbeth's "washing" the blood off her hands.

Occam's Razor   A principle, suggested by the mediaeval philosopher William of Occam, that has been accepted as fundamental to scientific explanation: if there are rival explanations for a given phenomenon the simplest must always be chosen. LLOYD MORGAN'S CANON is fashioned from the same metal as Occam's Razor.

occipital   Referring to the back of the BRAIN or skull.

occupational psychology   See WORK PSYCHOLOGY.

occupational therapy   An adjunct to PSYCHOTHERAPY in hospitals which involves patients in performing useful tasks to improve their SELF-ESTEEM and feelings of worth, as well as their physical condition.

Ockham's Razor   Alternative spelling of OCCAM'S RAZOR.

Oedipus complex   In Freudian theory, the notion that young boys desire their mother sexually and so experience rivalry with their father. See also ELECTRA COMPLEX.

oestrogen   The HORMONE secreted during the period of oestrus when the female animal experiences heightened sexual receptiveness. No such simple relationship beteween oestrogen and sexuality appears to be true of humans.

old brain   The most primitive part of the human BRAIN, which emerged earliest in the course of EVOLUTION. Situated below the CEREBRUM, it deals with REFLEX actions and basic bodily processes and contains the LIMBIC SYSTEM.

olfaction   The sense of smell.

one-trial learning   Learning that occurs after a single trial or practice.

one-way screen   A window into a room that looks like a mirror to the participant on the other side. Used by an observer in experimental studies of human and animal behaviour and in the training of PSYCHOTHERAPISTS.

ontogeny   The evolution and development of an individual organism. Contrast with PHYLOGENY.

operant conditioning   A form of LEARNING in which behaviour is controlled by the giving of reward or REINFORCEMENT. An extension of Thorndike's "INSTRUMENTAL LEARNING" theory. See SKINNER.

operational definition   Defining a concept in terms of the operations or techniques by which it can be studied.

operational diagnostic criteria   A set of standards that can be used to judge whether someone is suffering from a particular mental illness.

opinion leader   Denotes a person of status within a given group whose opinions are highly thought of and who can therefore influence the opinions of other members. See TWO-STEP FLOW OF COMMUNICATION.

opportunity sampling   Participants are selected because they are available, not because they are representative of a population.

optic array   In Gibson's theory, the pattern of light reaching the eye.

optic chiasm   The point at which the OPTIC NERVES from each eye cross over to the opposite side of the BRAIN.

optic flow patterns   Perceptual effect in which the visual environment appears to move away from the point towards which a person is moving.

optic nerve   The nerve that carries information from each eye to the BRAIN.

optimal foraging theory   An explanation of foraging in terms of achieving a balance between costs and benefits.

optimum level of arousal   An explanation of MOTIVATION that proposes that the animal has a DRIVE to return to an optimum state—that of moderate arousal.

oral stage   According to FREUD this is the first stage in an infant's life when he or she is mainly concerned with the pleasure received from his or her mouth and its functions. As with all Freud's stages, excessive frustration or satisfaction may leave a person fixated on it, with the eventual result that, in this case, as an adult the person may exhibit an oral character typified by a great need for oral stimulation in the form of food, drink, cigarettes, or even talking— especially perhaps when making "biting" comments.

ordinal data   Data that can be rank ordered from smallest to largest.

organising tendency   A term sometimes used in the study of PERCEPTION to describe the way INNATE physiological processes combine with experience to structure our perceptual world.

organisational culture   This term denotes "CULTURE" as used by both ANTHROPOLOGY and PSYCHOLOGY, i.e., that not only the shared beliefs, values, attitudes, and expectations of its members make up the culture of an organisation, but also the unquestioned assumptions about its traditions and ways of doing things.

orgone   Wilhelm Reich's concept of a life force, which is most clearly present at the time of sexual orgasm.

orienting reaction   Term used in PHYSIOLOGICAL PSYCHOLOGY to describe an animal's behaviour in altering its stance to deal with new stimuli in its environment.

osmoreceptors   Specialised NEURONS in the lateral preoptic area of the HYPOTHALAMUS that detect changes in osmotic pressure.

osmosis   The passage of a solution through a semi-permeable membrane into a more concentrated solution, i.e., one with higher osmotic pressure.

osmotic thirst   Thirst created as a consequence of increased solutes in the body. This increases the osmotic pressure outside the cells, thus creating intracellular water loss and changes in osmotic pressure that are detected by OSMORECEPTORS.

outcome measures   Ways of assessing the consequences of different forms of therapy.

outer-directed   A term introduced by David Riesman to describe people who respond to their society mainly by conforming to SOCIAL NORMS, by seeking approval and courting popularity.

outgroups   The groups to which an individual does not belong, often regarded unfavourably. Contrast with INGROUPS.

out-of-body experience   The feeling of a free-floating disembodied SELF detached from one's physical being, as reported for example by people who have been in a state of clinical death from which they have recovered. In such circumstances people frequently report looking down at themselves, lying on an operating table for instance.

overachiever   A person who exceeds the level of achievement expected of him or her. Sometimes used in the field of education to describe someone who tries too hard, i.e., a person whose ambitions appear to outstrip 'their abilities. Contrast with UNDERACHIEVER.

overcompensation   Producing a greater effort than is needed to overcome a difficulty or resolve a defect. Often used in connection with attempts to overcome an INFERIORITY COMPLEX.

overconforming   Sometimes used to describe a person who is excessively slavish to the demands of authority or the conventions of SOCIAL NORMS.

overdetermined   In PSYCHOANALYSIS, something that has more than one cause; used particularly about the origin of a NEUROSIS or the meaning of a DREAM. As most neuroses and most dreams are considered to be overdetermined, the process of analysis usually goes beyond the simple-minded search for a single explanation to complex phenomena.

over-extension Using words to apply to more objects than is strictly correct.

overlearning LEARNING in which practice or repetition continues beyond the point required for adequate mastery of the task. Overlearning is not usually considered harmful, i.e., it is not thought possible to learn something too well.

over-regularisation Applying grammatical rules to situations in which they do not apply.

P

paediatric Referring to childhood health and diseases.

paedophilia The sexual attraction of an adult to children.

paired associates A technique used in studies of LEARNING where words are presented to the participant in pairs and afterwards he or she is given the first word of each pair and asked to recall the second.

paleopsychology The study of psychological processes supposedly left over from an earlier stage of human EVOLUTION. For example, JUNG's suggestion of a COLLECTIVE UNCONSCIOUS.

palsy A form of paralysis often accompanied by trembling.

panic disorder with agoraphobia A disorder characterised by panic attacks and avoidance of open or public places.

paper-and-pencil test Any kind of test or PROJECTIVE TECHNIQUE that requires written answers.

papez circuit A BRAIN circuit or loop involved in EMOTION, based on the HYPOTHALAMUS, hippocampus, and thalamus.

paradigm According to Kuhn, a general theoretical orientation that is accepted by most scientists in a given discipline.

paradoxical sleep A term used to describe REM SLEEP because of the behavioural contradictions (paradoxes): eye movement, heart rate, breathing, etc. are increased but the body is in a state of near paralysis and it is difficult to wake a person up.

paradox of altruism   The paradox that altruistic behaviour has been naturally selected (as evidenced by the fact that it exists) despite the fact that such behaviour would appear to reduce the altruist's own survival and reproduction.

parakinesis   A term used in PARAPSYCHOLOGY to describe what appears to be the movement of objects by unknown powers.

paralanguage   Non-verbal signals, e.g., body language, eye contact.

paralinguistics   The study of the subtext of communication, e.g., pauses, pitch, body language, etc.

parallax   The PERCEPTION of objects as moving when the eyes are moved. Objects closer than the point the eyes are fixed on seem to move in the opposite direction from the eye movements; objects beyond the fixation point seem to move in the same direction as the eye movements. Near objects also appear to move more rapidly than distant objects. Parallax provides important cues in DEPTH PERCEPTION.

parallel distributed processing (PDP)   See CONNECTIONISM.

parameter   Mathematically, a constant in an equation that defines the form of the curve; in PSYCHOLOGY, it is a constant that defines the curve of a psychological function, like LEARNING. The term is sometimes used loosely, and wrongly, as if it was "perimeter".

parametric statistics   Statistics that deal with a NORMAL DISTRIBUTION.

paranoia   A PSYCHOSIS characterised by DELUSIONS, especially DELUSIONS OF GRANDEUR and DELUSIONS OF PERSECUTION. Apart from such delusions, which may be vigorously and even plausibly defended, a person suffering from paranoia can often behave quite normally.

paranormal   Psychological events that do not seem to be explainable by known scientific principles; the subject matter of PARAPSYCHOLOGY.

parapraxis   Apparent mistakes of behaviour like forgetting familiar names or slips of the tongue; known as FREUDIAN SLIPS in psychoanalytic thought.

parapsychology   The branch of psychology that deals with PARANORMAL phenomena as observed by EXTRASENSORY PERCEPTION. The task of parapsychology is to expand the known methods and principles of psychology to include an explanation of paranormal phenomena.

114

parasympathetic branch   The part of the AUTONOMIC NERVOUS SYSTEM that monitors the relaxed state, conserving resources, and promoting digestion and metabolism.

parental investment   The time and effort devoted by a parent to rearing its offspring.

Parkinson's Law   Work expands to fill the time available for its completion. Suggested by the British writer C. Northcote Parkinson.

partial reinforcement   See INTERMITTENT REINFORCEMENT.

participant observation   A research technique in the social sciences where an observer becomes an accepted member of the group he or she wants to study.

part method   A technique of LEARNING in which the material is broken down into smaller parts to be learned separately and then re-combined. Compare with WHOLE METHOD.

passive-aggressive personality   A person who expresses anger and hostility by oscillating between extreme dependence on, and extreme aggression towards, other people. The term passive-aggressive is also used of behaviour that is passively aggressive. For example, a person arriving late for a meeting with someone he or she knows will become anxious at their lateness.

paternalism   Treating adults like children by withholding from them the power to make decisions affecting their own lives.

pathological   ABNORMAL, in the sense of diseased or disordered.

patriarchy   A society or a social group run by men. Contrast with MATRIARCHY.

patrilineal   Applied to a society or social group where descent or inheritance is traced through the male line. Contrast with MATRILINEAL.

pattern recognition   Identifying two-dimensional patterns and three-dimensional objects in spite of variations in size and orientation.

Pavlov, Ivan (1849–1936)   Russian physiologist who won the Nobel prize for his work on the digestive system of dogs. In the course of his work he chanced upon a phenomenon he could not explain and followed it (reluctantly) out of physiology and into PSYCHOLOGY. What puzzled him was that his dogs began to salivate not only when they were presented with food but even before they were fed, when they recognised the man coming to feed them. The series of EXPERIMENTS he designed in an attempt to find the causes

115

of this behaviour became known as CLASSICAL CONDITIONING and Pavlov spent the last 30 years of his life working out the applications and the implications of his discovery. Although Pavlov thought he had found a way of studying the BRAIN, rather than behaviour, his work inspired a new American school of psychology called BEHAVIOURISM.

PDP See PARALLEL DISTRIBUTED PROCESSING.

peak experience In HUMANISTIC PSYCHOLOGY a rare moment of great emotional power in which a person feels something akin to ecstasy in being at one with themself and with the world. A moment of SELF-ACTUALISATION.

pecking order The hierarchy of status relationships formed among farmyard hens by their process of pecking each other. The most pecked hen has the lowest status. The term is now routinely (and therefore dangerously) applied to status relationships in human groups. Similarly, the term "hen-pecked" has long been part of everyday speech.

pediatric See PAEDIATRIC.

pedophilia See PAEDOPHILIA.

peer group A social group with which one associates on more or less equal terms. Used especially of childhood and ADOLESCENCE.

peer tutoring Teaching of one child by another, with the child doing the teaching generally being slightly older than the child being taught.

pellagra A nutritional deficiency whose most obvious symptom is a skin disease, but which may also be accompanied by psychological disorders, particularly DEPRESSION.

penis envy According to FREUD, penis envy is universal in women and leads (in the unconscious of course) to their CASTRATION COMPLEX. Not the most popular of Freud's theories among women.

penology The study of criminal behaviour and its treatment.

percentile In statistics, one-hundredth of the total number of scores in a ranked distribution. For example, the 90th percentile is the point below which lie 90% of the scores.

perception The process by which the BRAIN receives the flow of information about the environment from the sense organs and uses this raw material to help an organism make sense of that environment.

perceptual defence Defending oneself (one's SELF), or one's EGO from the awareness of unpleasant PERCEPTIONS by misperceiving them as being pleasant or inoffensive, or by not perceiving anything at all.

permissive amine theory   The view that mood disorders result from low levels of SEROTONIN leading to reduced control of NOR-ADRENALINE levels, both of which are NEUROTRANSMITTERS in the amine group.

perseveration   The tendency for an activity to recur even when there is no apparent stimulus and the activity has no obvious usefulness.

perseverative search   Mistakenly searching for an object in the place in which it was previously found, rather than the place in which it is currently hidden.

persona   From the Latin word for a theatrical mask; JUNG's term for those conscious, surface aspects of PERSONALITY that people employ in their everyday social dealings.

personality   Semi-permanent internal predispositions that make people behave consistently, but in ways that differ from those of other people.

personal space   In SOCIAL PSYCHOLOGY, the idea that the area immediately surrounding a person is felt to be his or her own. The amount of space claimed in this way varies from person to person and from CULTURE to culture, but any invasion of it is taken as a hostile or threatening act. Not to be confused with TERRITORIALITY.

person-oriented aggression   Aggression that has as its main goal harming another person.

person perception   The process by which people form impressions of others then flesh them out and make them coherent.

person variables   The ways that people differ, such as beliefs and cognitive abilities.

PET scan   A picture of BRAIN activity based on radioactive glucose levels within the brain; PET stands for "positron emission tomography".

Peter Principle   People are promoted to the level of their incompetence and stick there. Suggested by Canadian educational psychologist, Laurence Peter.

petit mal   See EPILEPSY.

PGR   Psychogalvanic reflex. American equivalent of the British GALVANIC SKIN RESPONSE.

phallic stage   According to FREUD this is the third stage in a child's life, between the ages of 3 and 7, when the child is mainly concerned with the pleasure received from his or her sex organs and their functions. As with all of Freud's stages excessive frustration or satisfaction may leave a person fixated on it so that, in this case, as an adult he or she may be preoccupied by sexual potency, performance, and conquest.

phallic symbol   Anything that can be taken as representing the phallus or penis such as a pencil, a church steeple, a cigarette, or a snake. The term phallus is used in ANTHROPOLOGY and mythology to describe the virtually universal representations of the male organ of generation. The idea of the phallic symbol was taken over into PSYCHOANALYSIS as an aid to DREAM INTERPRETATION, though pop psychologists and the general public have made much more of it than psychoanalysts ever did. Like other dramatic psychoanalytic ideas it cannot be used in a simple-minded way. Perhaps that is why JUNG is supposed to have suggested that "the penis is only a phallic symbol", and FREUD that "sometimes a cigar is really just a cigar".

phantasy   See FANTASY.

phantom limb   The sensation of "feeling" in a limb that has been amputated. Two complementary reasons for this phenomenon have been suggested; the existing SELF-IMAGE or body SCHEMA in an adult takes a long time to adjust to a sudden physical change, and the neural links built up between the amputated limb and the brain may still exist in some form.

phenomenology   An approach that emphasises subjective experience as the basis for understanding the world, as opposed to objective, external reality.

phenomenon   Anything that appears to an observer; anything that is capable of being perceived.

phenothiazines   NEUROLEPTIC DRUGS that reduce dopamine activity.

phenotype   The observable characteristics of an individual, resulting from the interaction between GENES and the environment. Contrast with GENOTYPE.

pheromones   Chemical substances produced by the body and secreted into the air. They act on CONSPECIFICS by being absorbed into their bloodstream. The pheromones then work like HORMONES.

phi phenomenon   The impression of seeing apparent movement. In its simplest form two lights flashed on and off in quick succession, with the right time interval between the flashes, will induce people to perceive the light as moving between two points. This ILLUSION is the basis for our PERCEPTION of movement in films, cartoons, and neon light displays. It was discovered at the beginning of the 20th century by the first GESTALT psychologists, shortly after the film industry was created.

phobia   A morbid NEUROTIC fear of a particular object or situation.

photographic memory   See EIDETIC IMAGERY.

phrenology   A pseudoscience which supposed that the bumps on the surface of the skull are related to function; the larger the bump the more developed the function.

phylogeny   The EVOLUTION and development of a species. Contrast with ONTOGENY.

physiognomy   Formerly referred to the attempt (now considered pseudoscientific) to divine psychological characteristics from the structure of the human face, a practice that sometimes included PHRENOLOGY. Now refers simply to the structure of the face.

physiological   Concerning the study of living organisms and their body parts.

physiological approaches to stress management   Techniques that try to control the body's response to STRESS by reducing physiological reactivity. For example, anti-anxiety drugs decrease the FIGHT OR FLIGHT RESPONSE such as high blood pressure, increased heart rate, etc. BIOFEEDBACK is another technique which works by training the participant to recognise their heightened physiological reactivity and reduce it through relaxation exercises.

physiological determinism   The view that behaviour is determined by internal, bodily systems.

physiological psychology   The branch of psychology that deals with the physiological processes underlying behaviour.

physiological reductionism   Explanations of complex behaviours in terms of simpler physiological (bodily) changes.

Piaget, Jean (1896–1980)   Swiss pioneer of DEVELOPMENTAL PSYCHOLOGY who postulated a series of sequential stages in the developing processes of COGNITION in children; these are the SENSORIMOTOR, PREOPERATIONAL, CONCRETE OPERATIONS, and FORMAL OPERATIONS stages. Piaget was trained as a biologist and retained this orientation throughout his work, believing that the developmental process in children should be allowed to run its own course

119

without encouraging a child to develop at a faster pace. Piaget began his career in psychology by administering INTELLIGENCE TESTS to children. He noticed that when children gave the wrong answers to his test questions they did so in a particular manner; all the children of a certain age gave the same kind of wrong answers to the same questions. By asking children questions about how they perceive things he was able to demonstrate that the world of the child is quite different from that of the adult, both separated from each other by a mutual incomprehension.

pictorial cues   Various MONOCULAR CUES to depth used by artists to create a three-dimensional impression.

pilot study   A smaller, preliminary study that makes it possible to check out standardised procedures and general design before investing time and money in the major study.

pineal gland   A very small endocrine gland located in the BRAIN that produces MELATONIN, and is involved in the CIRCADIAN RHYTHM.

PK   See PSYCHOKINESIS.

placebo   An inactive substance disguised as an active one, e.g., a sugar pill given to a CONTROL GROUP in a drug EXPERIMENT, or to a patient in hospital who would not benefit from an active drug but needs to feel that he or she is receiving treatment.

placebo effect   Positive responses to a drug or form of therapy based on the patient's belief that the drug or therapy will be effective, rather than on the actual make-up of the drug or therapy.

planning fallacy   The tendency to underestimate how long a work task will take to complete in spite of evidence from similar tasks completed in the past.

plantar reflex   The automatic curling downward of the toes when the sole of the foot is stroked; normally replaces the BABINSKI REFLEX at about the age of 2.

plateau   See LEARNING PLATEAU.

play therapy   The use of play in PSYCHOTHERAPY with children to aid in diagnosis and in treatment; the child is encouraged to experience a CATHARSIS of blocked EMOTIONS.

pleasure centre   An area of the HYPOTHALAMUS that apparently causes sensations of pleasure when electrically stimulated.

pleasure principle   The drive to do things that produce pleasure or gratification.

pluralistic ignorance   A situation in which each individual

120

believes themself to be the only exception to the accepted beliefs or behaviour of their group.

PNS (peripheral nervous system)   Part of the nervous system that excludes the BRAIN and spinal cord, but consists of all other nerve cells in the body. The PNS is divided into the somatic nervous system and the AUTONOMIC NERVOUS SYSTEM.

polyandry   A mating system in which one female mates with many males.

polygamy   A mating system in which one individual of one sex mates with many individuals of the other sex.

polygenetic inheritance   Behaviours, such as INTELLIGENCE, that are inherited through more than one GENE.

polygynandry   A mating system in which many males mate with many females (also known as PROMISCUITY).

polygyny   A mating system in which a male mates with several females, but females usually mate with only one male; parental care is usually provided by the female.

polymorphism   The process of passing through different bodily forms in the course of an organism's development, as in a frog or butterfly.

polymorphous perverse   In Freudian PSYCHOANALYSIS, the idea that the sexuality of a young child still passing through the ORAL, ANAL, and PHALLIC STAGES of development has no clear outlet, and that sexual pleasure derived from these sources would, if exhibited in an adult, be considered a perversion.

population   In STATISTICS, the total number of cases or individuals from which a SAMPLE is drawn for study and about which inferences are to be made.

positive correlation   When two co-variables increase at the same time.

positive reinforcement   Used in CONDITIONING as a way of increasing the strength of a given response by rewarding it.

positivism   The philosophical doctrine that scientific knowledge is limited to observed facts and experience.

possession   The feeling of being taken over by some external force. A common symptom of PSYCHOSIS in our CULTURE and religious ecstasy in others.

postconventional morality   The third level of the American psychologist Lawrence Kohlberg's stage theory of MORAL

121

DEVELOPMENT. At this level moral behaviour is governed neither by fear nor convention but by a self-chosen, consciously held system of rational ethical principles. Not everyone achieves this stage of development.

post-hypnotic suggestion A suggestion made to a person under HYPNOSIS which he or she carries out after coming out of the trance, supposedly without knowing the origin of the suggestion.

post-modernism The view that the detached objective observer—a key assumption in traditional Western science and scholarship—doesn't exist. In PSYCHOLOGY this takes the form of SOCIAL COGNITION and SOCIAL CONSTRUCTIONISM.

postpartum depression DEPRESSION following childbirth, perhaps due partly to hormonal changes.

pragnanz In GESTALT PSYCHOLOGY, the tendency of any gestalt towards simplicity, harmony, meaningfulness, and a "goodness of fit". For example, a battered old coin seen in a dim light will still be perceived as a circular object.

precognition A form of EXTRASENSORY PERCEPTION in which a subject appears to have knowledge or COGNITION of a future event which could not be inferred logically.

preconscious In PSYCHOANALYSIS, something that is not present in consciousness at a given moment but which can readily be recalled. Compare with SUBCONSCIOUS.

preconventional morality According to the American psychologist Lawrence Kohlberg, the first level of MORAL DEVELOPMENT which dominates the moral behaviour of children until after the age of 7. Preconventional morality is characterised by the PLEASURE PRINCIPLE of avoiding pain or punishment and seeking the pleasure of rewards for behaviour that adults judge to be morally good or bad.

predictive validity See CONSTRUCT VALIDITY.

prefrontal leukotomy A more precise form of PSYCHOSURGERY than the PREFRONTAL LOBOTOMY, which involves drilling two holes in either side of the skull and inserting needles to sever specific nerve fibres, thus effecting a functional removal of areas of the frontal lobes.

prefrontal lobotomy A form of PSYCHOSURGERY where the fibres running from the frontal lobes to other parts of the BRAIN are cut. Lobotomies typically make patients calmer but there are side-effects including apathy, diminished intellectual powers, impaired judgements, and even coma and death.

prejudice An ATTITUDE, which is usually negative, towards the members of some group on the basis of their membership of that group.

preoperational stage The second stage in PIAGET's theory of COGNITIVE DEVELOPMENT, from 2 to 7 years. The child can cope with symbols (such as using language) but cannot cope with adult internally consistent logic (operations).

preparedness The notion that each species finds some forms of learning more "natural" and easier than others.

presentation of self A term associated with the Canadian sociologist Erving Goffman. See IMPRESSION MANAGEMENT.

press Those environmental characteristics that are relevant to need-satisfaction.

pretest See PILOT STUDY.

prevision A term, very similar to PRECOGNITION, used in the study of EXTRASENSORY PERCEPTION to refer to the experience of "seeing" future events. Popularly known as "second sight".

primacy effect The high level of RECALL of the first items in a list in free recall; it depends mainly on extra rehearsal. Compare with RECENCY EFFECT.

primal scene In PSYCHOANALYSIS, the term for one's earliest sexual memory, which is usually taken to be the observation (partial, total, or fantasised) of one's parents in the act of intercourse.

primary attachments The earliest and most lasting bonds a human being makes with others.

primary colours Those colours that are used in combination to produce any other hue: blue, yellow, red, black, and white.

primary group A small group (such as the NUCLEAR FAMILY) characterised by direct, intimate personal relationships between people who depend on each other for support and for satisfaction of emotional needs.

primary motor cortex A region located in the frontal lobe of the CEREBRAL CORTEX that contains NEURONS that directly affect MOTOR NEURONS. The areas of the body are topographically represented.

primary process In PSYCHOANALYSIS, the UNCONSCIOUS attempts by the ID, governed by the PLEASURE PRINCIPLE, to find ways of obtaining immediate gratification of its needs.

primary reinforcers Rewarding stimuli that are needed to live (e.g., food; water).

principle of equipotentiality The view that all parts of the CEREBRAL CORTEX have the same potential.

principle of parsimony See OCCAM'S RAZOR.

prisoner's dilemma Situation developed from GAME THEORY and used in SOCIAL PSYCHOLOGY to study bargaining behaviour. In the game, two suspects are caught by the police and questioned separately about the crime. If one prisoner confesses and the other does not, the squealer is set free and the fall guy takes the rap. If both confess, both are convicted but dealt with leniently. If neither confesses, both benefit because they cannot then be convicted.

privation The lack of any ATTACHMENTS, as distinct from the loss of attachments (DEPRIVATION). This is due to the lack of an appropriate attachment figure. Privation is more likely than deprivation to cause permanent emotional damage or "AFFECTION-LESS PSYCHOPATHY"; the condition diagnosed by BOWLBY as involving permanent emotional damage.

proactive aggression Aggressive behaviour that is initiated by the individual in order to achieve some goal.

proactive interference Current LEARNING and MEMORY being disrupted by previous learning. Contrast with RETROACTIVE INTERFERENCE.

probability In statistics, the likelihood that a given event will occur as compared with the likelihood of alternative events occurring. For example, the probability of obtaining a given number when throwing six-sided dice is one in six.

problem space An abstract view of all the possible states that can occur, when solving a problem, between the start and the solution.

procedural knowledge Practical knowledge. A conscious "knowing how" to do something. Compare with DECLARATIVE KNOWLEDGE.

programmed learning A type of learning devised by SKINNER and based on OPERANT CONDITIONING, in which tasks are broken down into individual frames.

projection In PSYCHOANALYSIS, a DEFENCE MECHANISM where a person unconsciously attributes to other people feelings he or she has but which are too threatening to the EGO to admit into his or her CONSCIOUSNESS.

projective techniques Procedures for uncovering a person's UNCONSCIOUS MOTIVATIONS, ANXIETIES and conflicts. Like the RORSCHACH or the TAT they consist of relatively unstructured stimuli which are designed to encourage the projection of material that would be inadmissible to CONSCIOUSNESS in a direct undisguised form.

promiscuity See POLYGYNANDRY.

propositional representations One of the most widely used concepts in COGNITIVE PSYCHOLOGY. They have been called "the language of the mind" and are usually considered to be abstract linguistic symbols that together form a universal human code in which language and thought processes occur regardless of the native tongue actually used.

proprioceptors Sensory receptors that deal with information about the movement and orientation of the body. They are found in the SEMICIRCULAR CANALS of the inner ear where they are concerned with balance and in the muscles and joints where they produce KINAESTHETIC sensations.

pro-social behaviour Behaviour that is of benefit to others.

prosopagnosia A condition caused by BRAIN DAMAGE in which the patient cannot recognise familiar faces, but can recognise familiar objects.

protection of participants from psychological harm An ETHICAL GUIDELINE, which states that participants should be protected from psychological harm, such as distress, ridicule, or loss of SELF-ESTEEM. The risk of harm during the research study should be no greater than the participants would experience in their everyday life. DEBRIEFING can be used to offer support if a study has resulted in psychological harm.

protocol The steps used by a participant while carrying out a cognitive task (e.g., solving a problem). Often recorded by asking the person to speak their thoughts out loud.

prototype A typical example of something.

proximity See CONTIGUITY and CONTINUITY.

proximodistal Literally, "close-distant". Usually refers to the process of maturation in humans and animals where the sequence of physical development proceeds from the centre of the body towards the periphery. Compare with CEPHALOCAUDAL.

psyche The Greek term for the life force; translated first as "soul" then as "MIND" and now sometimes as "SELF".

psychedelic A term usually applied to drugs like HALLUCINOGENS which appear to sharpen PERCEPTION and expand CONSCIOUSNESS;

125

also used of colour and lighting arrangements that are supposed to have the same effects.

psychiatrist   A physician who specialises in PSYCHIATRY.

psychiatry   The branch of medicine concerned with mental illness. The subject matter of psychiatry overlaps to a great extent with that of CLINICAL PSYCHOLOGY, the main difference lying in the training and orientation of the PSYCHIATRIST and the clinical psychologist. The psychiatrist usually has no training in psychology other than in PSYCHOPATHOLOGY and is encouraged to adopt a MEDICAL MODEL for dealing with psychological disturbance. The clinical psychologist usually has no training in medicine, cannot prescribe drugs, and tends to regard normal and abnormal behaviour as being on the same continuum.

psychic   In general the properties of the MIND or PSYCHE; popularly used for a person supposedly possessing spiritual or EXTRASENSORY powers.

psychic determinism   The view that adult behaviour or PERSONALITY is predetermined by events in early childhood—a mix of biological and experiential factors.

psychical research   Popular term for PARAPSYCHOLOGY.

pychoactive drug   Any substance that alters mood, behaviour, or conscious mental processes. Technically this could include a nice cup of tea but the term is mainly reserved for the more dramatic results of using (and abusing) HALLUCINOGENS and PSYCHEDELICS.

psychoanalysis   FREUD's set of theories about human behaviour; also the form of treatment for mental disorders he devised.

psychoanalyst   A psychotherapist who has been trained in the theory and techniques of PSYCHOANALYSIS. He or she will have been trained initially as a physician, a psychiatric social worker, or a psychologist. A typical training programme may last for 4 years and will include a personal analysis of the trainee.

psychobabble   A term introduced in the 1970s by R. D. Rosen to describe a simple-minded quick fix, usually for an emotional need or problem, couched in pseudo-scientific terms with "a light dusting of psychology". My favourite is the Whole Brain Wave Form Synchro-Energizer. As the purpose of these quack remedies is the highly rational one of making money for their inventors they don't quite qualify as PSYCHOCERAMICS.

psychoceramics   The study of crackpot ideas about human behaviour.

psychodiagnostics Originally applied to the interpretation of PERSONALITY through external features like PHYSIOGNOMY and GRAPHOLOGY; now includes perfectly respectable PROJECTIVE TECHNIQUES.

psychodrama Technique developed by American psychiatrist J. L. Moreno. Used in both diagnosis and PSYCHOTHERAPY where a person is asked to act out certain scenes, usually in front of other patients and therapists. These scenes are designed to elicit the patient's personal and social conflicts.

psychodynamic model A model of ABNORMALITY based on the PSYCHODYNAMIC (psychoanalytic) approach which emphasises the influence of early experiences and of repressed EMOTIONS that are expressed unconsciously.

psychodynamics See DYNAMIC PSYCHOLOGY.

psychogenic Relating to a psychological disorder with no known organic basis.

psychohistory The application of psychological thought to the study of historical events and people. The field has been captured (in both the popular and the academic mind) by the attempted PSYCHOANALYSIS of leading historical figures. This psychobiography began with FREUD's own study of Leonardo Da Vinci and has had a controversial career ever since. However, many other lines of psychohistorical enquiry have also been opened up including the history of psychological concepts like *mind, insanity, the unconscious, the history of childhood, the social psychology of demographic movements*, and the attempt to unravel cause and effect in *the change of attitudes over time.*

psychokinesis In PARAPSYCHOLOGY, the supposed ability to move objects and affect the physical environment purely by the power of the MIND.

psycholinguistics The study of the relationship between the nature, structure, and use of language and the psychological processes of the users.

psychological altruism Altruistic behaviour resulting from cognitive rather than biological processes.

psychological approaches to stress management Techniques that try to control the cognitive, social, and emotional responses to STRESS. They attempt to address the underlying causes of stress, such as faulty thinking and disproportionate emotional responses (overreactions and underreactions). Psychological techniques work by changing the person's PERCEPTION of the STRESSOR and/or increasing the individual's perception of control.

127

psychological field   See LIFE SPACE.

psychological warfare   The application of psychological thought and research to the manipulation of ATTITUDES in wartime in an attempt to lower the enemy's morale and increase one's own.

psychologism   The view that all studies of human beings (philosophical, political, historical, etc.) should be based on PSYCHOLOGY, or even that all questions about human beings are reducible to psychology.

psychologist's fallacy   Where a psychologist reads into someone else's mind what is present in his or her own.

psychology   Most commonly defined at present as "the scientific study of mind and behaviour". No dictionary on the subject is content to leave it there, however, and one such volume (admittedly with claims to being "comprehensive") goes on and on about it for seven pages. But no definition of such an enormously wide-ranging subject will satisfy every psychologist. Indeed one dictionary claims that "psychology simply cannot be defined". My own opinion is that "the scientific study of mind and behaviour" most accurately describes the route to increasing our psychological *knowledge* (behaviour) while it focuses on a psychological *understanding* of what that behaviour is about and how to make sense of it (MIND). Both are essential.

psychometrics   Tests and measures of psychological factors including INTELLIGENCE TESTS.

psychomotor   Refers to the effects of mental processes on the actions of the muscles.

psychoneuroimmunology   The study of the effects of both STRESS and other psychological factors on the IMMUNE SYSTEM.

psychoneurosis   See NEUROSIS.

psychopath   See ANTI-SOCIAL PERSONALITY.

psychopathology   An area of PSYCHOLOGY in which the focus is on the nature of mental disorders and the factors that cause them to exist.

psychopharmacology   The study of the effects of drugs on psychological functioning.

psychophysics   The study of the relationship between external stimuli from the physical world and the subjective sensations they produce. The psychological processes involved are still as much a part of the subject matter of EXPERIMENTAL PSYCHOLOGY as they were when these problems were studied in the first psychological laboratories established in the 1870s. See WUNDT.

psychosis A psychological disorder that is severe enough to disrupt a person's everyday life and require institutional treatment. Apart from organic causes like BRAIN DAMAGE it has been thought by many psychologists that a psychosis is a severe form of NEUROSIS. More recently there has been a tendency to regard biochemical factors as being important in at least some forms of psychosis. It is characterised by a lack of contact with (other people's) reality.

psychosomatic From the Greek words *psyche* (MIND) and *soma* (body); relating to psychological disorders in which emotional STRESS produces physiological symptoms. Illnesses such as asthma and stomach ulcers are widely believed to be psychosomatic, but it has also been argued that because of the close connection between mind and body, every illness is psychosomatic at least to some extent.

psychosurgery Surgery where sections of the BRAIN are removed or LESIONS are made to treat a psychological condition.

psychotherapist Someone who practises PSYCHOTHERAPY. He or she is usually a PSYCHIATRIST, a clinical psychologist, or a psychiatric social worker but in many places where psychotherapy is practised no special qualifications are legally required.

psychotherapy The use of psychological techniques to treat psychological disturbances. The four main forms of psychotherapy (based on the four main theoretical approaches to PSYCHOLOGY) are BEHAVIOURAL, COGNITIVE, HUMANISTIC, and PSYCHOANALYSIS. There are many variants and permutations of these four approaches.

pubescence The stage of attaining puberty.

punctuated equilibrium The notion that long periods of relative stability for a species are punctuated by short-lived periods of rapid change.

punishment training A form of OPERANT CONDITIONING in which the probability of a response being made is reduced by following it with an unpleasant or aversive stimulus.

Purkinje phenomenon Named after a 19th-century Czech physiologist, this is the PERCEPTION that the red end of the spectrum decreases in visibility in decreasing illumination faster than the blue end of the spectrum. This is why blues seem more vivid than reds at sunset.

Pygmalion effect See ROSENTHAL EFFECT.

pyromaniac A person with a MANIA for lighting fires.

Q

Q sort A technique for rating PERSONALITY TRAITS in which a person is given a large number of statements about himself, herself, or someone else, which he or she then sorts into piles representing the degrees to which the statements are applicable.

qualitative change Change in how things are expressed, what it feels like, meanings or explanations; i.e., quality.

qualitative data Data generated using QUALITATIVE METHODS.

qualitative methods Research methods that are concerned more with the quality and richness of the data being collected than the control of the research situation, the quantity of data, or the sophistication of the statistical analysis of them available to the researcher. PARTICIPANT OBSERVATION and open-ended INTERVIEWS that do not use a detailed questionnaire are the most common examples in psychological research. Compare with QUANTITATIVE METHODS.

quantal hypothesis The idea that sensations are not a continuous experience but a succession of separate steps.

quantitative change Change in how much there is of something; i.e., quantity.

quantitative data Data that are concerned with quantity—how much. Data are presented in numerical terms and generated using QUANTITATIVE METHODS.

quantitative methods Research methods that are concerned more with the precision and generalisability of the data being collected than their richness of content, i.e., having a narrower but sharper focus than QUALITATIVE METHODS. The EXPERIMENT and the structured QUESTIONNAIRE are the most common examples in psychological research.

quartile One of the three points on a FREQUENCY DISTRIBUTION that divide it into equal quarters.

quasi-experiment Research that is similar to an EXPERIMENT but certain key features are lacking, such as the direct manipulation of the INDEPENDENT VARIABLE by the experimenter and random allocation of participants to conditions.

questionnaire survey A survey requiring written answers.

queuing Sometimes used to describe a way of dealing with sensory overload in which all the stimuli but one are put "on hold" until that one has been processed.

quiet sleep A term used to refer to NREM (non-rapid eye movement) sleep.

quota sampling Sampling data from each subgroup of a given population.

R

r The symbol for the most common CORRELATION COEFFICIENT.

race A term in ANTHROPOLOGY denoting a biological sub-division of human beings with a common genetic ancestry. This common ancestry produces common physical characteristics such as skin colour, facial structure, and size. There is no such thing as a pure race; every physical characteristic can be found, however infrequently, in every large human subgroup. It is suggested from time to time that a particular minority subgroup is inferior in INTELLIGENCE to the majority subgroup. A century ago it was Jews; more recently it has been Blacks. There has never been any clear evidence for this viewpoint and a lot of evidence against it. Even if we accepted for the sake of argument that there was a pure race and that INTELLIGENCE TESTS measured intelligence, those tests remain educationally, culturally, and socially biased against ethnic minority groups.

radical behaviourism The view that all behaviour is learned. B. F. SKINNER was a radical behaviourist.

random sampling Selecting participants on some random basis (e.g., numbers out of a hat). Every member of the population has an equal chance of being selected.

131

randomising In EXPERIMENTAL PSYCHOLOGY, the random selection of participants for an experimental group, or the random presentation of stimuli to the participants in the EXPERIMENT. This is done so that all individual factors are evened out and will not affect the experimental results.

range The difference between the highest and lowest score in any condition.

rank order A series arranged in order of magnitude either increasing or decreasing.

rapid eye movements See DREAM SLEEP.

rapport A kind of EMPATHY that a PSYCHOTHERAPIST has for a patient, supplemented by the confidence and trust that the patient has in the therapist. Rapport is essential for successful PSYCHOTHERAPY.

ratio data As INTERVAL DATA, but with a meaningful zero point.

rational-emotive therapy A form of COGNITIVE THERAPY developed by Albert Ellis that aims to produce rational thinking by aggressively challenging irrational beliefs.

rationalisation In PSYCHOANALYSIS, a DEFENCE MECHANISM where a person justifies behaviour about which he or she has UNCONSCIOUS GUILT feelings.

reactance theory A concept in SOCIAL PSYCHOLOGY which holds that people will react against attempts to curtail their choices and influence their decisions by finding the object of these restrictions ever more attractive, and by adopting an opposing viewpoint as a way of resisting pressure. See, for example, the ROMEO AND JULIET EFFECT.

reaction formation In PSYCHOANALYSIS, a DEFENCE MECHANISM where a person deals with UNCONSCIOUS DRIVES that he or she finds threatening by reacting consciously in the opposite direction. For example, men with strong homosexual tendencies that they are afraid of may behave in a very "macho" fashion.

reaction range Gottesman's solution to the NATURE–NURTURE DEBATE in which genetic make-up (GENOTYPE) sets some limit on the range of possible development. Actual development within this range (PHENOTYPE) is related to environmental opportunity.

reaction time The time elapsed between the presentation of a stimulus and the participant's response to it.

reactive aggression Aggressive behaviour that is produced in response to someone else's aggressive behaviour.

reactive depression   DEPRESSION resulting from external causes, as distinct from ENDOGENOUS DEPRESSION.

reality principle   FREUD's explanation for the motivating force of the EGO; it is a DRIVE to accommodate the demands of the environment in a realistic way.

reality testing   In PSYCHOANALYSIS, the EGO's practical attempts to follow the REALITY PRINCIPLE.

recall   Retrieving, and being able to reproduce, information from MEMORY. Compare with RECOGNITION.

received pronunciation (RP)   A form of spoken English used by educated, middle-class individuals in southern England.

recency effect   Good free RECALL of the last few items in a list based on information in the SHORT-TERM MEMORY store. Compare with PRIMACY EFFECT

receptor   A sensory nerve ending that responds to a particular kind of stimulus; found in the sense organs and the surface of the skin.

recessive gene   A GENE that remains latent because it is paired with a DOMINANT GENE.

recidivism   Mainly used to describe recurrent criminal behaviour but also used of repeated psychological disturbance.

reciprocal altruism   A form of mutual benefit where a selfless act is performed with the expectation that the favour will be returned at a later date. Such behaviour is ADAPTIVE as long as cheating doesn't occur.

reciprocal determinism   Bandura's concept that what one learns is affected by one's characteristics (PERSONALITY, beliefs, and cognitive abilities). Personality isn't simply determined by the environment, but the individual also shapes the environment.

reciprocal punishment   The view that the form of punishment should fit the crime.

reciprocity   See DELAYED RECIPROCAL ALTRUISM.

recognition   Identifying information previously seen, read, or heard about and stored in the MEMORY. Compare with RECALL.

reconstructive memory   This is a form of RECALL that involves an active process whereby the MEMORY is reassembled with some pieces of "real" information and some pieces that are "made up" to fill in the gaps in memory. The gaps are filled in based on our existing knowledge and experience of the world, called SCHEMAS. Schemas include STEREOTYPES, PREJUDICES, and our expectations of

133

the world. Consequently, the memory recalled is not an accurate reproduction of the original stimulus; it is distorted by the schemas that have filled in the gaps.

recovered memory Memories apparently brought into conscious awareness, from the UNCONSCIOUS where they have been REPRESSED, through HYPNOSIS or the suggestion of a PSYCHOTHERAPIST. These memories are often of early sexual abuse and in any given case might be accurate, but they are widely regarded as unreliable by themselves because of the ease with which FALSE MEMORIES can be constructed.

redintegration A principle that is taken to be a prime example of the LAWS OF ASSOCIATION where the PERCEPTION of a whole unit is accomplished after only a part of it has been presented to the subject.

reductionism The notion that PSYCHOLOGY can ultimately be reduced to more basic sciences such as physiology or biochemistry.

reference group A term in SOCIOLOGY for a group with which a person identifies and whose GROUP NORMS that person follows, whether he or she is accepted by it or not, and whether he or she is physically part of it or not. Compare with MEMBERSHIP GROUP.

reflex An INNATE and automatic response to a stimulus.

regression Returning to earlier stages of development when under severe STRESS.

rehearsal The verbal repetition of information, which strengthens its MEMORY TRACE or ENGRAM.

reification Treating an abstract idea as though it had a real objective existence.

reinforcement A behaviour is more likely to re-occur because the response was agreeable. Both POSITIVE and NEGATIVE REINFORCEMENT have agreeable consequences.

relative deprivation A gap between what we have done (and had) and what we expected to be able to do (and have).

relative morality This is based on the notion that the acceptability of any act depends in part on the benefits that it produces; in other words, the ends can justify the means.

releaser In ETHOLOGY, a stimulus that releases an automatic behavioural response in an organism. See also INNATE RELEASING MECHANISM.

reliability The extent to which a method of measurement or a research study produces consistent findings across situations or over time.

REM sleep See DREAM SLEEP.

repeated measures design A research design where the same participants are used for all conditions in the EXPERIMENT.

repetition compulsion The compulsion to repeat the same behaviour over and over again, the classic example being Lady Macbeth's hand washing.

replicability A feature of research, in which the findings of an EXPERIMENT can be repeated.

representativeness heuristic "Rule of thumb" enabling judgements to be made on the basis of PROBABILITY.

representative sample A sample that is intended to be completely representative of the POPULATION from which it is drawn.

repression This is a DEFENCE MECHANISM suggested by FREUD whereby memories that cause ANXIETY are kept out of conscious awareness as a means of protecting the individual. This is also called "motivated forgetting". An example of this could be when you do not want to do something particularly tiresome (such as homework!) and so you forget all about it.

research The process of gaining knowledge and understanding via either theory or EMPIRICAL data collection.

research hypothesis A statement put forward at the beginning of a study stating what you expect to happen, as generated by a theory.

resistance In PSYCHOANALYSIS, resistance is the term that describes both the reluctance of material submerged by REPRESSION in the UNCONSCIOUS to surface into CONSCIOUSNESS and the reluctance of the analysand, or patient, to allow the analyst's probing to uncover areas of unconscious conflict.

resistant attachment (type C) An insecure attachment of an infant to its mother. The child resists contact on reunion.

resonance Gibson's explanation for how we detect invariant sensory information; the information is there in the environment and one simply tunes into it.

response bias A MENTAL SET to respond in a particular way to certain issues or questions, for example on a QUESTIONNAIRE.

restricted code In Bernstein's theory, concrete and descriptive language. Contrast with ELABORATED CODE.

retina   The inner surface of the eyeball which receives visual images and transmits them as neural impulses via the OPTIC NERVE to the BRAIN.

retrieval   Recovering stored information. Essentially, remembering it.

retroactive interference   Subsequent learning disrupting MEMORY for previous learning. Contrast with PROACTIVE INTERFERENCE.

retrograde amnesia   The inability to recall the events leading up to the TRAUMA that induced the AMNESIA.

retrospective falsification   Unintentional distortion in remembering previous experiences which is not thought to be caused by UNCONSCIOUS influences.

right to withdraw   The basic right of participants in a research study to stop their involvement at any point, and to withdraw their results if they wish to do so.

risky shift   A form of GROUP POLARISATION where people make riskier decisions under the influence of a group than by themselves. The opposite of CAUTIOUS SHIFT.

ritualisation   The evolutionary process by means of which signals come to be more effective at communicating information to other animals; ritualised signals tend to be STEREOTYPED, exaggerated, and repetitive.

rods   Photoreceptors in the RETINA that are specialised for vision in dim light and for detection of movement.

Rogers, Carl (1902–1987)   A leading exponent of HUMANISTIC PSYCHOLOGY and NON-DIRECTIVE THERAPY of which his own CLIENT-CENTRED THERAPY is a leading example.

role   Used in SOCIAL PSYCHOLOGY to refer to the kind of behaviour expected of a given person in a given situation.

role playing   Used in two senses; acting the part of another person in a therapeutic or experimental situation, or playing a ROLE for deliberate effect.

role taking   The ability to watch the behaviour of another individual and understand their intentions.

Romeo and Juliet effect   An experimental finding in SOCIAL PSYCHOLOGY that parental opposition can lead to the strengthening of a young couple's love.

rooting reflex   The automatic response of an infant to having its cheek stroked; turning its head and opening its mouth.

Rorschach test   The most famous of all PROJECTIVE TECHNIQUES. It consists of ten standardised inkblots developed by Herman Rorschach, a Swiss PSYCHIATRIST. The subject's FREE ASSOCIATION to the inkblots is examined by the tester in the light of certain categories of response which have been standardised over many years. No diagnosis of a person's difficulties would ever be made solely on the basis of a Rorschach test but many CLINICAL PSYCHOLOGISTS still regard it as a useful first step.

Rosenthal effect   A form of EXPERIMENTER BIAS or SELF-FULFILLING PROPHECY in a social setting, suggested by Robert Rosenthal. Rosenthal led a group of teachers to believe that certain children in their classes had high IQs and were expected to do well in the year ahead. The children did do well—although they were all in fact of average IQ.

rote learning   Learning solely through repetition without any attempt to find meaning or order in the materials.

runaway process   Fisher's theory that some inherited characteristics become more and more exaggerated because females actively select mates with this feature. Also called the "SEXY SONS HYPOTHESIS".

S

saccadic movement   The jumping of the eye from one point of fixation to another, as in reading.

sadism   The experience of sexual pleasure through inflicting physical pain. Usually considered a sexual perversion. Named after the Marquis de Sade who did it for a living.

sado-masochism   The tendency towards both SADISM and MASOCHISM at the same time. FREUD held that they were, in effect, two sides of the same coin.

salience   That aspect of a situation or behaviour that is especially prominent or conspicuous.

sample   A group of cases or individuals studied as representatives of the POPULATION from which they are drawn. See also BIASED SAMPLE and RANDOM SAMPLING.

satyriasis   An obsession with sex in men; the male equivalent of NYMPHOMANIA.

scaffolding   The context provided by an adult or other knowledgeable person which helps the child to develop his or her cognitive skills.

scapegoat   The object of displaced aggression. In Biblical times the Israelites sent a white goat out to die in the wilderness once a year, on the Day of Atonement, carrying the sins of the people with it.

scattergraph   Two-dimensional representation of all the participants' scores in a CORRELATIONAL ANALYSIS; also known as scattergram.

schemas   Organised packets of information stored in LONG-TERM MEMORY.

schizoid   Relating to SCHIZOPHRENIA.

schizophrenia   A severe condition in which there is a loss of contact with reality, including distortions of thought, EMOTION, and behaviour.

scripts   Sets of SCHEMAS that guide people when performing commonplace activities, such as going to a restaurant or catching a bus.

search image   A mental representation of an object that assists in RECOGNITION, for example, the visual features of a prey.

Seashore test   A series of recorded tests of musical abilities developed by the American psychologist Carl Seashore.

seasonal affective disorder   A disorder that nearly always involves the sufferer experiencing severe DEPRESSION during winter months.

secondary reinforcer   A stimulus that is rewarding because it has been associated with a PRIMARY REINFORCER; examples are money and praise.

second-order conditioning   See HIGHER-ORDER CONDITIONING.

secure attachment (type B)   A strong contented bond between the infant and caregiver. The secure infant shows distress at SEPARATION but is easily comforted by the caregiver when reunited. This characterises the majority of attachments and is related to healthy development as the infant has a positive working model of relationships.

selective attention   The deliberate focusing of attention on something to the exclusion of competing stimuli.

selective pressure   In evolutionary terms, the pressure of competition to reproduce successfully in the face of limited resources.

self The self, in HUMANISTIC PSYCHOLOGY, is roughly the equivalent of the EGO in PSYCHOANALYSIS. It refers to that part of the PERSONALITY that is conscious of its IDENTITY over time.

self-actualisation The need to discover and fulfil one's potential.

self-concept All the elements that make up a person's view of himself or herself, including SELF-IMAGE.

self-disclosure Revealing personal information about oneself to someone else.

self-discovery An active approach to LEARNING in which the child is encouraged to use his or her initiative in learning.

self-efficacy An individual's assessment of his or her ability to cope with given situations.

self-esteem How well a person likes themself; how worthy he or she deems themself to be.

self-fulfilling prophecy The idea that expectations concerning one's own or other people's behaviour can lead to the expected behaviour appearing, such as in the ROSENTHAL EFFECT. See also EXPERIMENTER BIAS.

self-image The SELF a person believes himself/herself to be. One's self-image is a composite of many things and may bear little relation to any *objective* assessment of oneself or the assessment of others. The self-image begins very early in life and is probably, to a large extent, physical. The judgements of other people are also important in the formation of the self-image.

self-regulation A process of self-reward if an internal standard of performance is achieved, but feelings of failure if it is not achieved.

self-serving bias The tendency to take the credit for one's successes, but not to accept blame for one's failures.

semantic coding ENCODING or processing words in terms of their meaning based on information stored in LONG-TERM MEMORY.

semantic differential A technique developed by the American psychologist Charles Osgood for assessing the way in which the same words or ideas are understood by different people. Participants are asked to rate these terms along dimensions like good–bad or active–passive and these ratings are then compared.

semantic memory Organised knowledge about the world and about language, stored in LONG-TERM MEMORY.

semicircular canals Three fluid-filled canals that are located in the inner ear at right-angles to each other and pass information about movement and balance to the BRAIN.

senescence A term sometimes used in DEVELOPMENTAL PSYCH-OLOGY to focus attention on the psychological STRESSES and conflicts of old age and the AGEING process as well as the unique and positive aspects of being old.

senile dementia Name given to DEMENTIA found in old people whose symptoms are often referred to as "senility". It is a degenerative condition and includes, for example, the later stages of ALZHEIMER'S DISEASE.

sensation Experience following the stimulation of a sense organ, like the eyes or ears, and a necessary prerequisite to PERCEPTION.

sensitive period A looser interpretation of the concept of a CRIT-ICAL PERIOD—changes are more likely during the period of time rather than being exclusive to it.

sensitivity training A technique for trying to improve inter-personal communication and the quality of relationships in small groups. Derived from HUMANISTIC PSYCHOLOGY and based on the methods and experience of GROUP THERAPY. Group leaders try to facilitate open and honest discussion of feelings within the group. The hope is that any new-found sensitivity to one's dealings with other people will carry over to other areas of life.

sensorimotor stage The first stage in PIAGET's theory, at which children learn to co-ordinate their sensory and motor abilities.

sensory buffer An early part of the processing system, in which information stays for a short period of time before being attended to or disappearing from the system.

sensory deprivation A situation where people are deprived of the usual stimulation of their senses encountered in daily life. When people are isolated from sensory stimulation, as far as possible, in a laboratory they quickly become bored and then start to experience HALLUCINATIONS.

sensory memory The first stage of the MEMORY process, lasting less than a second, during which information is recorded by the sense organs. See SHORT-TERM MEMORY and LONG-TERM MEMORY.

separation This refers to the absence of the caregiver (e.g., due to work commitments, divorce, or hospitalisation), which usually causes great distress, but not necessarily permanent bond disruption. Separation has a number of effects, such as protest, despair, or detachment, and if prolonged it may result in DEPRIVATION.

separation anxiety   The sense of ANXIETY felt by a child when separated from their ATTACHMENT figure.

separation protest   The infant's behaviour when separated— crying or holding out their arms. Some insecurely attached infants show no protest when left by their ATTACHMENT figure, whereas securely attached children do.

serendipity   From the island of Serendip in *Gulliver's Travels*; the experience of finding one thing while looking for another; true in varying degrees of major figures in the study of the human condition, like FREUD and PAVLOV. Also found in users of dictionaries.

serial learning   Learning material in a particular order or sequence.

serial reproduction   A method used by Bartlett to show how information changes as it passes between different people. Bartlett read a story to an individual, who then told their version to another participant, who in turn passed the information on to the next participant, and so on. This method allows us to see what changes take place with each reproduction.

seriation   A child's ability to arrange objects in order on the basis of a single feature (e.g., height).

serotonin   A NEUROTRANSMITTER that is associated with lower arousal, sleepiness, and reduced ANXIETY.

servomechanism   A system that controls another system. FEED- BACK from the system under control enables the servomechanism to regulate its input so that a constant output is maintained. A thermostat is a common example of a servomechanism but HOMEOSTASIS in the body can also be seen as such.

set point   The ideal or most appropriate value of the SYSTEM VARIABLE.

sex   The biological fact of being male or female as determined by a pair of CHROMOSOMES.

sex differences   Differences in behaviour or abilities between males and females. There may not be many. For instance, what looks like a genetic sex difference in aggressiveness is due to a CULTURAL process of LEARNING which gender role is considered appropriate for males or females.

sex-linked trait   A genetically transmitted characteristic that is found more frequently in one sex than the other. Perhaps the clearest example is that of red–green COLOUR BLINDNESS which is far more common in men than women.

141

sexual identity   Maleness or femaleness based on biological factors.

sexual selection   Selection for characteristics that increase mating success.

sexy sons hypothesis   The notion that females mate with the most attractive males so that their own sons will inherit these characteristics and thus be attractive to other females. Related to the RUNAWAY PROCESS.

shadowing task   A task in which one auditory message is repeated back out loud while another auditory message is ignored.

shame culture   A CULTURE that relies on shaming and ridiculing by others to regulate the behaviour of individuals and thus maintain order and social control. Such a culture is vulnerable to people not getting caught when breaking rules, if there is no internalised mechanism of self-regulation. Contrast with GUILT CULTURE.

sham rage   A kind of cool aggression that was displayed in cats after ABLATION of their CEREBRAL CORTEX.

shaping   A form of OPERANT CONDITIONING in which responses need to become closer and closer to what is desired in order to be rewarded.

shell shock   The First World War equivalent of what is now known as COMBAT FATIGUE or BATTLE FATIGUE.

shibboleth   A Hebrew word whose pronunciation was used by one of the ancient tribes of Israel as a password and is used now to denote evidence of one's being "in the know" or belonging to an "in" group.

shock treatment   See ELECTROCONVULSIVE THERAPY.

short-term memory (STM)   A temporary place for storing data where they receive minimal processing. Short-term memory has a very limited capacity and short duration, unless data in it are maintained through REHEARSAL.

sibling rivalry   Competition between children in a family, usually for the affection of the parents.

signal detection theory   An alternative to the concept of an ABSOLUTE THRESHOLD of sensation which suggests that PERCEPTION (detection) of a stimulus (signal) is related to the sensitivity of the sense receptors and the motivation of the individual to respond.

significant other   Denotes a person who is particularly important to us, especially in relation to our SELF-IMAGE. Compare with GENERALISED OTHER.

situational attributions Deciding that people's actions are caused by the situation in which they find themselves rather than by their PERSONALITY.

Skinner, B. F. (1904–1990) The most celebrated exponent and populariser of BEHAVIOURISM. His technique of OPERANT CONDITIONING was based on the work of PAVLOV, Thorndike, and WATSON. He expounded the social implications of his views in a number of influential works intended for the general public, notably *Walden Two* and *Beyond Freedom and Dignity*.

Skinner box The name given to the apparatus used by B. F. SKINNER in his studies of OPERANT CONDITIONING. The box must have some mechanism, like a bar or lever, which allows the animal being conditioned to manipulate or *operate* on its environment.

sleep centre An area of the HYPOTHALAMUS that induces sleep when it is electrically stimulated or removed entirely by surgery.

sleep deprivation When people are prevented from sleeping they eventually experience ill effects such as HALLUCINATIONS and confusions of thought and behaviour. Some scientists engaged in DREAM research argue that dreaming is the most important aspect of sleeping and therefore sleep deprivation. Other than dreaming it is difficult to detect any physiological difference between sleeping and just resting.

sleeper effect A term used in several different senses in the SOCIAL PSYCHOLOGY of ATTITUDE change. Its most frequent usage is probably in describing a change in an attitude or opinion after a study has been conducted. This may be one reason for inaccuracy in public opinion polls. The term is also used to describe a more favourable response to a communication after some time has elapsed, rather than the expected decline in the effect of the communication. It is also used to describe the dissociation between communication and communicator over time so that people may become less receptive to positive sources and more receptive to negative ones.

slip of the tongue See PARAPRAXIS.

sneak copulation Mating by a non-dominant male when the dominant male is not looking.

social anthropology The study of social systems and CULTURES in different societies, particularly non-literate societies.

social causation hypothesis The view that SCHIZOPHRENIA may be related to the greater STRESS experienced by members of the lower class, whereas middle classes have less stressful lives.

social cognition A combination of COGNITIVE PSYCHOLOGY and SOCIAL PSYCHOLOGY which emerged in the 1960s. Seen as part of the COGNITIVE REVOLUTION but with much older roots in GESTALT PSYCHOLOGY. Principally concerned with our INFORMATION PROCESSING and how we use it with the minimum expenditure of cognitive effort to make sense of our social environment and our social behaviour. This includes our ATTRIBUTION of social behaviour and causality, the way we STEREOTYPE people, and our use of HEURISTICS.

social cohesion The attraction that a group has for each of its members that helps to bind it together.

social comparison The process of evaluating one's ATTITUDES and behaviour by comparing them with those of other people. In SOCIAL PSYCHOLOGY there is an idea that when people are uncertain of what to do (or think or feel) in a given situation they are more likely to take their cue from other people and conform to their behaviour.

social constructionism An approach to PSYCHOLOGY based on the assumption that our knowledge of ourselves and of others is a social construction, and thus there is no objective reality for research.

social contract This describes an unwritten contract between people that is difficult to break because of social pressure. Thus, having agreed to take part in a study or to help someone, it is difficult to withdraw.

Social Darwinism The application to human societies of DARWIN's evolutionary theories of NATURAL SELECTION, where only the fittest members of a species survive. In effect it is an attempt to justify the existing order by arguing that the rich and successful have evidently been selected by nature to be rich and successful.

social deprivation Where an individual or a group does not have the material benefits common to a given society. The objective aspect of RELATIVE DEPRIVATION.

social development The development of the child's social competence includes social skills, ability to relate and empathise with others, and formation of close and meaningful relationships. Social development is determined by an interaction of biological predisposition and the environment.

social distance scale An attempt to measure the degree of social intimacy a person will accept in relation to other groups or individuals.

social drift hypothesis   The view that more people with SCHIZO-PHRENIA are members of the poorer classes, not because of the SOCIAL CAUSATION HYPOTHESIS, but because they drift into that group due to their inability to cope.

social exchange theory   See EXCHANGE THEORY OF FRIENDSHIP.

social facilitation   The enhancement of an individual's perform-ance when working in the presence of other people.

social identities   Each of the groups with which we identify pro-duces a social identity; our feelings about ourselves depend on how we feel about the groups with which we identify.

social identity theory   The idea that we readily divide people into INGROUPS and OUTGROUPS and that we find ingroups attractive because belonging to them enhances our SELF-ESTEEM. See also SOCIAL COMPARISON.

social influence   The influence of a group (majority influence) or individual (MINORITY INFLUENCE or obedience) on the thinking, ATTITUDES, and/or behaviour of others. For example, fashion trends are a consequence of majority influence; political and religious leaders are an example of minority influence; and com-plying with the demands of an authority figure, such as an employer, is an example of obedience.

social interaction   The mutual influence that people have on each other's behaviour in a social setting.

socialisation   The process whereby an individual becomes a social being. Although it is a lifetime process it is particularly important in childhood when society is represented by (and through) a child's parents and the rest of his or her family (Figure 14).

social learning theory   The view that behaviour can be explained in terms of both direct and indirect (VICARIOUS) REINFORCEMENT; indirect reinforcement and identification lead to IMITATION.

social loafing   The tendency of people to work less hard on a task when part of a group than as individuals, due to a DIFFUSION OF RESPONSIBILITY.

social marking   Conflict between an individual's cognitive under-standing and a social rule.

social norms   The standards or rules of behaviour for individuals expected by a given society or CULTURE.

social penetration theory   The theory that the development of a relationship involves increasing SELF-DISCLOSURE on both sides.

145

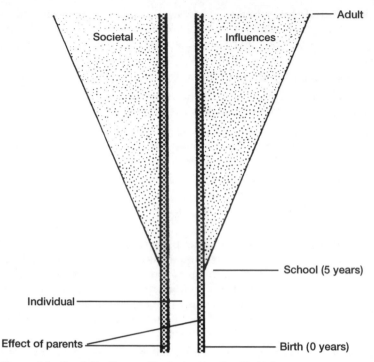

Figure 14 Socialisation as illustrated by the Statt Cone

social perception How we use data from our environment to perceive our social world.

social psychology The branch of PSYCHOLOGY that deals with social life, the behaviour of people in groups, and the behaviour of individuals in social settings.

social representations Knowledge about the world that is derived from social dialogues.

social science Any field of study concerned with people as social beings; to a greater or lesser extent these are generally considered to include ANTHROPOLOGY, economics, history, political science, PSYCHOLOGY, and SOCIOLOGY. (See Figure 3.)

social skills training A form of therapy based on the behavioural approach that involves teaching appropriate social skills by using rewards, MODELLING, and CONDITIONING.

social status Someone's position in society in relation to, and as determined by, other people.

146

social stratification   The division of a society into well-defined social classes.

sociobiologists   Scientists who argue that the roots of social behaviour are to be found in biological and genetic factors.

sociobiology   An approach to explaining social behaviour in terms of evolutionary processes; with special emphasis on the GENE as the unit for NATURAL SELECTION.

sociocentric   Regarding one's own society as superior to any other and the measure of all things good. It is similar to ETHNOCENTRISM and usually involves EGOCENTRISM.

socio-cognitive conflict   Intellectual conflict produced by exposure to the differing views of others.

socio-emotional leader   The individual who emerges in a small group as the person who keeps up the morale and facilitates the interpersonal relationships of the group. Compare with TASK LEADER.

sociolinguists   Scientists who argue that language functions in a social context and it is important to study it in this context.

sociology   The study of society in general and social organisation in particular.

sociopathic personality   See ANTI-SOCIAL PERSONALITY.

Sod's Law   If something can go wrong it will.

soft determinism   The notion that we should distinguish between behaviour that is very constrained by the situation (i.e., determined) and behaviour that is only modestly constrained (i.e., less exactly determined).

somatic therapy   A form of treatment for mental illness involving manipulations of the body (e.g., drug treatment).

somatising   Used in PSYCHOTHERAPY to describe the appearance of physical symptoms as a result of psychological stress, as in PSYCHOSOMATIC ILLNESS.

somatosensory area   A region located in the parietal lobe of the CEREBRAL CORTEX that receives information from various senses about temperature, pain, and pressure. The areas of the body are topographically represented.

sour grapes reaction   Convincing yourself that something you can't have is not worth having anyway. In CLINICAL PSYCHOLOGY it is called RATIONALISATION; in SOCIAL PSYCHOLOGY it is an attempt to resolve COGNITIVE DISSONANCE.

147

spaced practice   Any LEARNING with a time interval between practices but which does not necessarily distribute the practices to maximum advantage in the time available, as does DISTRIBUTED PRACTICE.

spatial memory   MEMORY for the layout of one's environment.

speaking in tongues   See GLOSSOLALIA.

speciesism   Discrimination and exploitation based on differences between species.

speech accommodation theory   The theory that people modify the way they speak to suit the context.

speech centre   An area of the BRAIN particularly associated with the ability to speak. See also BROCA'S AREA and WERNICKE'S AREA.

split-brain patients   Individuals who have had the fibres connecting the two CEREBRAL HEMISPHERES severed. This is done to reduce epileptic attacks in cases of severe EPILEPSY and involves severing the cerebral commissures that include the CORPUS CALLOSUM. People who have undergone this operation lose the ability to integrate sensations from both halves of the body and to coordinate the movements of limbs on both sides. There is no communication between the two halves of the BRAIN. It appears as though each half takes on the functions of the whole brain, resulting in two separate and independent brains and a double MIND. These effects are entirely the results of the operation and have *nothing whatever* to do with psychological phenomena like DUAL, MULTIPLE or SPLIT PERSONALITY or SCHIZOPHRENIA.

split personality   See MULTIPLE PERSONALITY.

spontaneous recovery   The re-emergence of responses over time following experimental extinction.

spontaneous remission   Recovering from an illness (or experiencing reduced symptoms) as a consequence of the passage of time rather than any treatment.

SQ3R   A long-established study method to aid textbook LEARNING, consisting of five strategies for effective reading (*S*urvey the material generally, *Q*uestion the issues it contains, *R*ead the material thoroughly, *R*ecite key points and *R*eview the material again).

squid magnetometry   A technique for assessing the magnetic flux or field in the BRAIN using a superconducting quantum interference device.

stage theory   A theory, such as that of PIAGET, that conceives of a developmental process taking place in a series of non-arbitrary, sequential, and progressive steps, each of which subsumes all the preceding steps.

standard deviation A measure of the spread of the scores around the MEAN. It is the square root of the VARIANCE and takes account of every measurement.

standardised tests Psychological tests that have been used with large groups of individuals in order to establish a set of "standards" or NORMS.

Stanford–Binet The American revision of the BINET SCALE, originally done at Stanford University in 1916 and now the most commonly used individual INTELLIGENCE TEST in the English language.

state dependency The reliance on a match of emotional or physical state at the time of an event and at the time of retrieval as a cue to RECALL.

statistical infrequency/deviation from statistical norms Behaviours that are statistically rare or deviate from the average/statistical NORM as illustrated by the NORMAL DISTRIBUTION curve, are classed as ABNORMAL. Thus, any behaviour that is atypical of the majority would be statistically infrequent, and so abnormal (e.g., SCHIZOPHRENIA is suffered by 1 in 100 people and so is statistically rare).

statistical significance The level at which the decision is made to reject the NULL HYPOTHESIS in favour of the EXPERIMENTAL HYPOTHESIS.

statistical tests Various formulae that enable you to analyse and compare data produced in research studies. A statistical test produces a statistic that can then be assessed, using tables of significance, to see if the data fit or do not fit the HYPOTHESIS.

statistics A form of mathematics used on data gathered in studying behaviour and by which investigators evaluate their findings and make inferences of wider implication than their study SAMPLE.

stereoscopic vision The PERCEPTION of depth or distance usually due to the merging of the two slightly different images that appear on the RETINA of each eye.

stereotactic neurosurgery A refined method of PSYCHOSURGERY that requires only a small opening to be made in the patient's skull, under local ANAESTHESIA.

stereotaxic Being able to precisely locate areas of the BRAIN, for example to enable an electrode to be placed there to record brain activity.

stereotype A SOCIAL PERCEPTION of an individual in terms of some readily available feature, such as skin colour or GENDER, rather than their actual personal attributes.

stimulus enhancement Where an animal may notice a stimulus in their environment because of the behaviour of another animal.

stimulus generalisation See GENERALISATION.

STM See SHORT-TERM MEMORY.

strabismus A squint, produced by lack of coordination of the eye muscles which does not permit both eyes to focus on the same point.

stranger anxiety The distress experienced by a child when approached by a stranger.

strange situation An experimental procedure developed by Mary Ainsworth and used to test the security of a young child's ATTACHMENT to a caregiver. It involves the child being placed in situations of increasing STRESS, to which his or her emotional reactions are carefully observed. The key features are what the child does when it is left by the caregiver and the child's behaviour at reunion, as well as responses to a stranger.

stratified sample A frequently used technique for mass polling. It involves the division of a POPULATION into subgroups and undertaking RANDOM SAMPLING of each subgroup.

stream of consciousness A term introduced by the American psychologist William James, whose brother Henry is considered to be the first writer of "stream of consciousness" novels. Intended to emphasise the continuous nature of one's conscious experience, as opposed to a contemporary trend in PSYCHOLOGY to divide CONSCIOUSNESS into separate units for study.

stress A state of psychological and physical tension produced, according to the transactional model, when there is a mismatch between the perceived demands of a situation (the STRESSOR[S]) and the individual's perceived ability to cope. The consequent state of tension can be ADAPTIVE (eustress) or maladaptive (distress).

stress inoculation training A technique to reduce STRESS through the use of stress-management techniques and self-statements that aims to restructure the way the client thinks.

stress management The attempt to cope with STRESS through reduction of the stress response. This may be aimed at the physiological effects of stress (e.g., anti-anxiety drugs or BIO-FEEDBACK) and the psychological effects of stress (e.g., STRESS INOCU-LATION TRAINING or HARDINESS training). Stress management is often based on changing the person's perception of the STRESSOR and/or increasing the individual's PERCEPTION of control.

stressor An event that triggers the STRESS response because it throws the body out of balance and forces it to respond. For example, LIFE CHANGES (e.g., divorce, bereavement), daily hassles (e.g., traffic, lost keys), workplace stressors (e.g., role strain, lack of control), and environmental stressors (e.g., noise, temperature, overcrowding). Stressors are not objective in that they do not produce the same response in all people, as this depends on the individual's PERCEPTION of the stressor. Thus nothing is a stressor unless it is thought to be so!

stroboscopic effect A visual ILLUSION of movement produced by a rapid succession of stationary images, as in films. (See PHI PHE-NOMENON.) The term is more specifically used of the effect obtained when a moving object is illuminated by a rapidly flashing light.

stroking Used in TRANSACTIONAL ANALYSIS of acts that demonstrate caring recognition of and attention paid to anther person. Analogous to the physical stroking of an infant.

Strong Vocational Interest Blank A QUESTIONNAIRE about a person's interests, which is matched with the reported interests of people in difference vocations.

structuralism A school of PSYCHOLOGY, closely associated with WILHELM WUNDT, which emphasises the contents of the MIND as it appears to INTROSPECTION and the mental framework or structure that contains these contents. Contrasted with FUNCTIONALISM.

subconscious Something that is not quite conscious but can readily be made conscious. The term is most often used in a physiological sense, to denote an area of the continuum running from full conscious awareness to deep sleep. Its PSYCHOANALYTIC equivalent is the PRECONSCIOUS, but *not* the UNCONSCIOUS with which it is popularly confused.

subcortical Those parts of the frontal region of the BRAIN that are not part of the CEREBRAL CORTEX. They lie "under" the cortex.

subculture Usually denotes a CULTURE within a culture, which shares the main features of the parent culture while retaining special characteristics of its own.

subjective Usually used to refer to something existing inside oneself and not capable of being experienced by others. Contrasted with OBJECTIVE.

subliminal   Referring to stimuli below the LIMEN or threshold of conscious PERCEPTION.

sublimination   In PSYCHOANALYSIS, a DEFENCE MECHANISM in which unacceptable UNCONSCIOUS impulses are channelled into consciously acceptable forms. For FREUD this was society's main way of handling REPRESSION. It is certainly the most socially acceptable of the defence mechanisms.

Summerhill   The school dedicated to freedom from REPRESSION founded by A. S. NEILL.

superego   In FREUD's theory, the part of the MIND concerned with moral issues.

superordinate goal   In SOCIAL PSYCHOLOGY, a goal that is beyond the capacity of any one group by itself, requiring the active cooperation of more than one group. Regarded as a means of promoting good relations between groups.

suprachiasmatic nucleus   A small group of NEURONS in the HYPOTHALAMUS that act as a BIOLOGICAL CLOCK and help regulate the CIRCADIAN RHYTHM.

surrogate   Someone who takes the place of another, psychologically. For example, an older sister as a mother surrogate, or a PSYCHOTHERAPIST as a father surrogate. In PSYCHOANALYSIS, the term is often used of someone or something, usually represented unconsciously in a DREAM, whose function is to conceal the true IDENTITY of the person or object causing powerful feelings.

survey research   A technique of gathering data from large numbers of people by the use of QUESTIONNAIRES and taking SAMPLES.

survival value   Referring to a physical or behavioural characteristic that increases the probability of survival of an individual or a species.

symbiosis   Biological term for the permanent dependence of two organisms on each other for their mutual survival. Sometimes used more loosely by psychologists to describe two people whose relationship appears to foster their individual NEUROSES. See also FOLIE A DEUX.

symbolic interaction   A sociological way of approaching SOCIAL PSYCHOLOGY. It emphasises the part played by language, gestures, and other symbols of SOCIAL INTERACTION in our conscious attempts to form ourselves and our world, and it regards our human qualities as the products of that social interaction.

sympathetic branch The part of the AUTONOMIC NERVOUS SYSTEM that activates internal organs.

sympathy The ability to feel *with* someone. An emotional experience, as opposed to EMPATHY.

symptom An indicator of an underlying PATHOLOGICAL condition.

symptom substitution When one symptom is eliminated, but the underlying problems lead to its replacement with another symptom.

symptom–syndrome approach Dealing with illness (physical or psychological) by identifying SYMPTOMS, diagnosing a SYNDROME, and suggesting a suitable form of treatment.

synaesthesia The experience of having sensations in a different MODALITY from the one being stimulated, e.g., "seeing" music in colour.

synapses The extremely small gaps between adjacent NEURONS.

syncretic thought A kind of thinking where new experiences are assimilated into rather vague and global SCHEMAS. Syncretic thought occurs because young children focus on two objects at a time, and find it hard to consider the characteristics of several objects at the same time. It is characteristic of the PREOPERATIONAL STAGE.

syndrome A set of SYMPTOMS that are generally found together.

synopticity A synopsis is a survey or outline that draws together common threads. The various approaches in PSYCHOLOGY such as BEHAVIOURISM and the biological approach, and issues such as REDUCTIONISM and ETHICAL ISSUES, are common threads that run through the whole of psychology, i.e., they are synoptic.

systematic desensitisation A form of treatment for PHOBIAS, in which the fear response to threatening stimuli is replaced by a different response such as muscle relaxation.

systems theory A system is usually considered to be a series of interconnected elements forming an organised or organic whole, e.g., CENTRAL NERVOUS SYSTEM or KINSHIP SYSTEM. Systems theory attempts to formulate general principles about all systems by a comparative analysis of their structures and functions.

system variable The characteristic that needs to be regulated in order to maintain a reasonably constant environment.

T

taboo A term in ANTHROPOLOGY for behaviour that is forbidden by a CULTURE. Usually has magical or religious associations, but often used in a wider context for any important social prohibition. In PSYCHOANALYSIS it often refers to the REPRESSION of socially unacceptable sexual impulses, like INCEST.

tact A form of language LEARNING in which saying a word almost correctly leads to a reward.

task leader The individual who emerges in a small group as the person who tries to keep the attention of the group focused on its task and who tries to see that the job gets done. Compare with SOCIO-EMOTIONAL LEADER.

TAT See THEMATIC APPERCEPTION TEST.

teaching machine An instrument for aiding PROGRAMMED LEARNING.

technophobia A PHOBIA about technology.

telegraphic period The second stage of language development, during which children use nouns and verbs in their speech, but tend to leave out other parts of speech.

telekinesis See PSYCHOKINESIS.

telepathy Communication between two MINDs, or knowledge by one person of another's thought, without the aid of the known senses. A form of EXTRASENSORY PERCEPTION.

temperament hypothesis The view that a child's temperament is responsible for the quality of ATTACHMENT between the child and its caregiver, as opposed to the view that experience is more important.

tender-minded A description by the American psychologist William James of one side of a PERSONALITY dimension (the other being TOUGH-MINDED). It implies an idealistic, optimistic, and spiritual kind of outlook.

territoriality The concept, developed mainly in ETHOLOGY, that certain animals will stake out territory, which they will defend, for their own use or the use of their group. The suggestion is that this tendency is INNATE in these animals. Behaviour that appears to be similar in humans should be labelled with great caution. There is no evidence that such behaviour is innate in human beings. See also CROWDING BEHAVIOUR.

test of association A type of STATISTICAL TEST where a calculation is made to see how closely pairs of data vary together, i.e., how close the association or CORRELATION is between them.

test of difference A type of STATISTICAL TEST where two sets of data are compared to see if they differ significantly.

testosterone A male HORMONE.

T-group A form of SENSITIVITY TRAINING.

thanatology From THANATOS, FREUD's term for the death force; the study of the way people deal with death and dying.

thanatos The Greek word for death, which FREUD adopted for his concept of the death force or death instinct; a tendency towards self-destruction. Contrasted with EROS.

Thematic Apperception Test (TAT) A PROJECTIVE TECHNIQUE developed by the American psychologist Henry Murray containing ambiguous and vague drawings (usually of one or more human figures) about each of which the subject has to make up a story. The themes that may emerge from these stories are then used to diagnose areas of emotional conflict or concern in the subject.

Theory of Mind Having an understanding that others' thoughts and emotions are different from one's own.

theory of naïve psychology The theory that people behave like naïve scientists who relate observable behaviour to unobservable causes.

therapeutic community A situation in which the total social environment is seen as aiding a patient to overcome psychological disturbance, on the basis that it was the patient's former total environment that led to his or her disturbance in the first place.

therapy See PSYCHOTHERAPY.

Third Force A term used for those psychologists who subscribe neither to a PSYCHOANALYTIC nor a BEHAVIOURIST view of the human condition but to a broadly HUMANISTIC one.

thought-disorder A disturbance of a person's usual thought processes; often taken as one symptom of PSYCHOSIS.

threshold See ABSOLUTE THRESHOLD and JUST NOTICEABLE DIFFERENCE.

tip-of-the-tongue phenomenon The failure to recall something we know well, which is on the "tip of the tongue". Due to a failure of retrieval from LONG-TERM MEMORY storage rather than the REPRESSION of painful memories.

T maze The simplest form of maze, in the shape of a letter "T".

token economy Institution-based therapy based on the principles of OPERANT CONDITIONING. Desirable behaviours are encouraged by the use of selective reinforcements.

tolerance for ambiguity The ability to live with a situation that is not clear-cut, where different interpretations of what is happening are possible and where the outcome is uncertain; the ability to accept complexity in human affairs without seeking simplistic solutions. High tolerance of ambiguity is usually seen as a sign of psychological health and maturity.

top-down processing Processing that is affected by expectations and prior knowledge, as distinct from BOTTOM-UP PROCESSING, which is driven directly by the stimulus.

topological psychology A form of FIELD THEORY by KURT LEWIN focusing on the interaction between an individual and his or her LIFE SPACE.

totem A term in ANTHROPOLOGY for a living thing, or a symbolic representation of it, which is worshipped by a group of people as a protecting spirit.

tough-minded A description by the American psychologist William James of one side of a PERSONALITY dimension (the other being TENDER-MINDED). It implies a materialistic, pessimistic, and unspiritual kind of outlook.

trace decay The physical disappearance of a MEMORY TRACE or ENGRAM.

tracking Making the necessary adjustments to follow a moving object; often used of an infant's eye movements or those of a patient with suspected BRAIN DAMAGE.

tradition-directed A term introduced by David Riesman to describe people who respond to their society mainly by following the rules and customs laid down in its traditions.

training analysis The analysis of someone training to be a PSYCHOANALYST.

trait Any enduring characteristic of a person.

transactional analysis A form of GROUP THERAPY in which the interrelationships of the group members are analysed in terms of their transactions with each other as "parent", "child" or "adult".

transcendental meditation A technique to reach an ALTERED STATE OF CONSCIOUSNESS achieved by relaxation and meditation on a MANTRA.

transference In PSYCHOANALYSIS, the transfer of the patient's strong feelings for one or both parents on to the therapist.

transfer of training Where the LEARNING achieved in one situation is transferred to another situation. This can be positive (knowing Spanish aids the learning of Italian) or sometimes negative (knowing how to steer a car is detrimental to steering a boat with a tiller). See LEARNING SET.

transformational grammar Noam Chomsky's concept of an INNATE set of rules for combining words to produce meaning.

transgenerational effect If a woman has, e.g., a poor diet during pregnancy, her foetus suffers and may be less able to reproduce future generations.

transitivity Understanding the relation between elements, for example x is greater than y and y is greater than z, therefore x is greater than z.

transsexuality Someone's feelings that he or she is really a member of the opposite sex in the wrong body. Transsexuals are the people who request sex change operations. Not to be confused with TRANSVESTISM.

transvestism The compulsion to dress in the clothes of the opposite sex or the experience of sexual excitement when dressed as a member of the opposite sex. Not to be confused with TRANSSEXUALITY.

trauma Physical or psychological shock resulting from injury or violence.

treatment aetiology fallacy The mistaken belief that the effectiveness of a form of treatment indicates the cause of a disorder.

trepanning Cutting holes in the skull so that the devils thought to cause mental illness can escape. It is still used to relieve pressure inside the cranial cavity.

trial and error learning The step-by-step LEARNING over many trials characteristic of most animal learning and much human learning, and the basis for CONDITIONING procedures. A very laborious process compared to INSIGHT LEARNING.

triangular theory of love Sternberg's theory that love has three components: intimacy, passion, and decision/commitment.

157

triangulation   A term borrowed from mathematics to describe the way in which research findings can be confirmed by looking at findings from other studies.

truth drug   A narcotic (like sodium amytal) that has the effect of causing drowsiness and reducing INHIBITION (and possible REPRESSION) so that the subject may reveal information that he or she would not do if fully conscious.

t-test   In statistics, a test for deciding whether the MEANS of two groups of scores are significantly different.

tutorial training   A traditional approach in which the teacher imparts knowledge to fairly passive students.

two-step flow of communication   The idea that the mass media of communication first influence the OPINION LEADERS in a community who in turn influence the opinions and attitudes of others.

Type A personality   In biopsychology, a PERSONALITY type who is typically impatient, competitive, time-pressured, hostile, and particularly subject to STRESS.

Type I error   Mistakenly rejecting the NULL HYPOTHESIS in favour of the ALTERNATIVE HYPOTHESIS when the results are actually due to chance.

Type II error   Mistakenly retaining the NULL HYPOTHESIS when the ALTERNATIVE HYPOTHESIS is actually correct.

U

ultradian rhythm   A biological rhythm that recurs in a cycle of less than a day (*"ultra"* and *"dies"* = above or higher frequency than a day); e.g., the sleep stages.

unconditional positive regard   In CARL ROGERS' CLIENT-CENTRED THERAPY, this is the attitude of total acceptance that the therapist has to show the client for the therapy to be successful.

unconditioned reflex   See UNCONDITIONED RESPONSE.

unconditioned response   A REFLEX or a response that has not been learned previously; so called when produced by a given stimulus at the beginning of the CONDITIONING procedure. For example, the unconditioned response of salivation in response to food may be used to induce salivation in response to a bell.

unconditioned stimulus A stimulus that produces an UNCONDITIONED RESPONSE at the beginning of the CONDITIONING procedure. For example, food producing salivation.

unconscious The most important concept of DYNAMIC PSYCHOLOGY and in particular of PSYCHOANALYSIS; the region of the PSYCHE that contains impulses and desires that are too threatening to be allowed into CONSCIOUSNESS and from which they have been repressed or inhibited from entering. The effects of this REPRESSION and INHIBITION are expressed in consciousness as NEUROTIC behaviour. FREUD systematically probed the dynamic mechanisms involved in its relationship with the conscious psyche and did more than anyone to expose the great amount of irrationality in human affairs.

unconscious motivation Any MOTIVATION of whose origin, or even existence, a person is unaware.

underachiever A person who fails to meet the level of achievement expected of him or her. Sometimes used in the field of education to describe someone who doesn't try hard enough, i.e., a person whose abilities could take them beyond their ambitions. Contrast with OVERACHIEVER.

under-extension Using words to apply to fewer objects than is strictly correct.

uniformitarianism The notion that biological and other processes operate in the same constant way over time.

utilitarianism The philosophy that the practical usefulness of something is the sole criterion of its value, a philosophy that has greatly hindered the advance of understanding in the study of human behaviour.

V

validity The extent to which something is true. This may be applied to a measurement tool such as a psychological test, where the soundness of the test (the extent to which it is measuring something that is real or valid) is being considered. It can also be used of the "trueness" of an experimental procedure both in terms of what goes on within the EXPERIMENT (INTERNAL VALIDITY) and its relevance to other situations (EXTERNAL VALIDITY).

variable   A condition or factor, usually in an EXPERIMENT, that is capable of changing or being changed.

variance   In statistics, the square of the STANDARD DEVIATION; used to measure the spread of scores in a particular test or experiment.

verbal deprivation theory   Bernstein's theory that language development is determined by social environment, and this affects COGNITIVE DEVELOPMENT. See ELABORATED CODE and RESTRICTED CODE.

verbal learning   Learning the uses of words.

vicarious reinforcement   The concept in SOCIAL LEARNING THEORY that REINFORCEMENT can be received indirectly, by observing another person being reinforced.

vicarious trial and error   A term in BEHAVIOURISM to describe the substitution of mental trial and error for physical trial and error in animals who stop at a decision point in a maze. It is an attempt to get round the difficulty that the animals appear to be thinking, a strict TABOO to a strict behaviourist.

Vigotsky test   See VYGOTSKY TEST

visual agnosia   A condition where individuals can see but fail to be able to recognise objects.

visual cliff   An apparatus used to study the existence of DEPTH PERCEPTION in human and animal infants. Its purpose is to produce the optical ILLUSION that part of the floor falls away sharply, to see whether the infant will have the depth perception necessary to be convinced by the illusion and refuse to venture off the "cliff" (Figure 15).

visual constancies   An object's size, shape, colour, and so on, are perceived as remaining fairly constant or unchanging in spite of large variations in the RETINAL image.

visual cortex   The part of the CEREBRAL CORTEX dedicated to vision, located in the OCCIPITAL lobes.

visual dominance   If we receive conflicting stimuli from different sensory MODALITIES, vision is usually the dominant one.

visual search   A task in which a visual target or targets must be located as quickly as possible from among distractors.

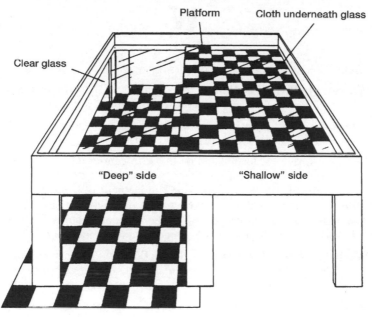

Figure 15   Visual cliff

visual spatial coding   The MEMORY's way of automatically encoding information by its appearance.

visuo-spatial sketch pad   A system within WORKING MEMORY designed for spatial and/or visual coding.

volunteer bias   The idea that volunteers for a study are atypical participants because their self-selection means they will probably be more highly motivated to perform well than people selected at random. This bias therefore casts doubt on any generalisation made from such a SAMPLE to a larger POPULATION. This is also a standard weakness of phone-in polls or magazine QUESTIONNAIRES asking for people's views on some issue.

voyeurism   From the French *voyeur*, literally "looker"; someone who gains most sexual pleasure from watching sexual activities or activities associated with sex, like undressing.

VTE   See VICARIOUS TRIAL AND ERROR.

Vygotsky test   A test of the ability to form concepts which involves sorting a series of blocks by colour, shape, and size; named after a leading Russian psychologist, a pioneer in studying the relationship of thought and speech to intellectual development.

W

WAIS See WECHSLER ADULT INTELLIGENCE SCALE.

Watson, J. B. (1878–1958) The founder of BEHAVIOURISM who later left academic life for a lucrative career in advertising.

weapons effect An increase in aggressive behaviour caused by the mere sight of weapons (e.g., hand guns).

Weber's Law As formulated by the 19th-century German physiologist, this was one of the first products of PSYCHOPHYSICS. The law concerns the relativity of one's judgement of stimulus sensations, stating that the JUST NOTICEABLE DIFFERENCE between two stimuli is a constant proportion of the original stimulus. This law holds good only for the middle range of stimulus intensities.

Wechsler Adult Intelligence Scale (WAIS) One of the most widely used INTELLIGENCE TESTS for adults combining performance and verbal ability testing.

Wechsler–Bellevue Scale See WECHSLER ADULT INTELLIGENCE SCALE.

Wechsler Intelligence Scale for Children (WISC) A modification, for use with adolescents and older children, of the WECHSLER ADULT INTELLIGENCE SCALE. (The STANFORD–BINET is the test most widely used with younger children.)

Wernicke's Area Named after Carl Wernicke, a 19th-century German neurologist. A vaguely defined area of the CEREBRAL CORTEX that is concerned with the processing of speech sounds into recognisable language.

whole method A technique for LEARNING in which the material is learned as a whole on each practice or repetition. Compare with PART METHOD.

WISC See WECHSLER INTELLIGENCE SCALE FOR CHILDREN.

wish-fulfilment In PSYCHOANALYSIS, an attempt to fulfil an impulse or desire, usually by FANTASY and in dreams.

withdrawal Removing oneself from a situation of conflict or ANXIETY and seeking refuge elsewhere such as in alcohol, drugs, sex, or even work.

withdrawal symptoms The physical and pyschological effects of no longer taking a substance to which one has become addicted.

Originally applied to hard drugs but now often used to describe negative reactions to virtually anything from giving up cream cakes to the end of the football season.

wolf boy   See FERAL CHILD.

word association test   A technique for probing areas of psychological difficulty that a person may have repressed. The subject is asked to give immediate responses to a list of pre-selected words while his or her answers and the time taken to react to each stimulus word are noted.

working memory model   A model of MEMORY proposed by Baddeley and Hitch as an alternative to the MULTI-STORE MODEL. The model consists of a CENTRAL EXECUTIVE (an attentional system, which has a limited capacity, and which is involved in decision making), together with two slave systems (the ARTICULATORY-PHONOLOGICAL LOOP, and VISUO-SPATIAL SKETCH PAD). This model is concerned with both active processing and the brief storage of information.

working through   A process of PSYCHOTHERAPY, and in particular PSYCHOANALYSIS, in which the patient goes over and over his or her basic problems with the therapist until the patient gains some insight into their origins and dynamics and achieves the ability to cope with similar situations unaided.

workplace stressor   Factors in the work environment or aspects of the job that cause STRESS. For example, overcrowding, noise, and temperature are factors in the environment. Lack of control, interpersonal relationships, ROLE ambiguity, and work overload are all examples of work pressures that cause stress.

work psychology   The branch of psychology that deals with the world of work. It includes selection, training, job satisfaction, the environment, the organisation, human relationships in the job, and ERGONOMICS.

Wundt, Wilhelm (1832–1920)   The first self-proclaimed psychologist, as opposed to physiologist or philosopher, who in the 1870s founded the first experimental laboratory. The programme of research now called PSYCHOPHYSICS and followed by experimental psychologists was intended to support his STRUCTURALISM theories. But it is often said that 20th-century psychology became dominated by BEHAVIOURISM and PSYCHOANALYSIS as a reaction against Wundt's thinking.

X

x and y chromosomes The CHROMOSOMES that determine sex. In most species, including *homo sapiens*, females have two x chromosomes and males one x and one y.

xenophobia A PHOBIA about strangers

Y

Yerkes–Dodson law The CURVILINEAR RELATIONSHIP between arousal and performance; when AROUSAL LEVEL is very low or very high, performance is poor. Performance is highest at a medium level of arousal.

Young–Helmholtz theory The best known theory of COLOUR VISION which suggests that the RETINA contains three types of colour receptors for red, green, and blue and that all other colours perceived are reducible to some combination of these three.

Z

Zeigarnik effect Finding by GESTALT psychologist Bluma Zeigarnik that participants are more likely to remember details of experimental tasks during which they were interrupted than those they were allowed to complete. The effect has been claimed for many everyday situations where someone is interrupted.

Zeitgeber German term meaning "time giver". Refers to external events that partially determine biological rhythms. For example, light is a zeitgeber in the CIRCADIAN RHYTHM.

Zeitgeist German term meaning "spirit of the times". Used to denote the prevailing social and political mood of an era, the conventional wisdom, the fads and fashions in everything from hair length to psychology. A zeitgeist affects the emotional and mental life of everyone who lives through it and is thought to have similar

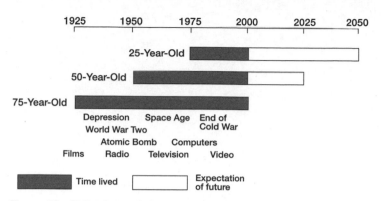

Figure 16 Zeitgeist and changes over time

effects on people of a similar age group, thus providing one basis for a GENERATION GAP. See also COHORT EFFECT. (Figure 16.)

zero-sum game In GAME THEORY, a situation where one person's losses are another's gains because there is a finite amount to be won (The gains and losses in the game add up to zero.) This situation has been suggested as a MODEL for the distribution of rewards in our society.

Zollner illusion A visual ILLUSION in which parallel lines appear to diverge.

zone of proximal development In Vygotsky's theory, capacities that are being developed but are not as yet functioning fully.

zoom-lens model The notion that visual attention is a spotlight with an adjustable beam.

zoomorphism The interpretation of human behaviour in terms appropriate to animal behaviour.

zoophobia A PHOBIA about animals.

zygote In humans and higher animals, the cell formed by the union of the sperm cell and the egg cell of the parents and from which a new individual will develop.